# Using
# GPS

# Using
# GPS

## Conrad Dixon

Second Edition

SHERIDAN HOUSE

Published 1999 by Sheridan House Inc.
145 Palisade Street
Dobbs Ferry, NY 10522

First edition 1994
Second edition 1999

*Library of Congress Cataloging-in-Publication Data*

Dixon, Conrad
    Using GPS / Conrad Dixon, -- 2nd ed.
      p.   cm.
    Includes index.
    ISBN 1-57409-059-3
    1. Global Positioning System. 2. Boats and boating. I. Title.
VK562. D69  1999
623. 89'3 -- dc21                        98-46569
                                          CIP

Printed in Great Britain

ISBN 1-57409-059-3

# Contents

## *Acknowledgments*

I am most grateful for the help given by Terry Johns, whose knowledge of the electronics industry is encyclopaedic, and to Professor Floriano Papi of the University of Pisa for supplying the photograph of Adelita, the turtle fitted with a transmitter. Sets were made available by Louise Holvey and Anna Tarnowski of Raytheon, Brian Ash of Mantsbrite Marine Electronics, Kevin Turner and Steve Walker of Eagle and Sylvie Callas of Garmin. Many sincere thanks for your help.

# 1 • How GPS Works

The Global Positioning System, whose full title is the Navstar Global Positioning System, is a satellite-based radio-navigation network that provides fixes in all parts of the world at all times of the day and night. Developed from research done at Johns Hopkins University in the late 1950s and then operated by the US Department of Defense, it is based on a space segment of 26 satellites in circular orbits about 10,900 miles above the earth's surface. These satellites are so spaced that at least five of them are in theoretical view of any user of the system at any one time. Each satellite goes round the world twice a day in one of six planes and transmits data continuously in one of two digital codes. The control segment consists of a master station at Colorado Springs and a number of monitor stations that track the satellites and act as conduits for information.

The purpose of this information exchange is to get satellites sending accurately-timed signals to receivers – to your GPS set. The time interval is about six-hundredths of a second. Atomic clocks in the satellites record the time a signal is sent out and less accurate ones at the receiving end note the time of receipt. The computer part of the GPS set turns the time interval into a distance or range, thus creating a position line, and puts several such position lines together to make a fix. It then displays the result as a latitude and longitude.

Three position lines obtained in this way give what is called a 2D fix; four give a 3D fix which takes account of the height of the antenna and provides reference timing. Height is generally constant in the case of marine craft and the figure goes in when installation and initialization takes place, but use at home, on high ground or by aircraft, entails telling the set how far it is above sea level to get the geometry right. The working of GPS is outlined in Figure 1 where a 'birdcage' of orbits and satellite vehicles encloses the earth and a fix from three ranges appears on it. Satellites look a little like cotton reels flanked by playing cards, and the latter element is the framework for solar panels that provide operating power.

Technically-minded readers may care to know that transmission times are recorded in nanoseconds (each one a thousandth of a millionth of a second), and that atomic clocks in satellites have about one second of error in seventy thousand years. Transmission takes place on 1575.42 MHz and 1227.6 MHz, with the first-named wavelength carrying what are called pseudo-random code messages for civilian use. The pseudo-random codes give the time interval between transmission and reception, and Figure 2 shows how the receiving set, marked with an R, compares the message from the satellite with an internally-generated version to get the time difference – the TD. This difference is converted to a range, so that – as with radar – intersecting arcs of range provide a fix.

**SOURCES OF ERROR**

The speed of radio signals, which is the same as the speed of light, is only constant in a vacuum, and messages tend to slow down as they pass through the ionosphere about 100 miles above the earth. A similar delay takes place as signals pass through the atmosphere where water vapour has a braking effect. Fortunately, these factors only give a few metres of error, but the angles of intercept are more significant. Plotting conventional bearings on a chart gives the best results when the lines of bearing are at right angles, and the same applies to satellite ranges where wide-spaced satellites give better results than those close together. It is all a matter of geometry, and it can be helpful to know when results are likely to be good. Figure 3 gives good and bad geometry side by side, and in the interests of clarity, only two satellites are shown although three is the minimum number to achieve a fix.

The expressions Horizontal Dilution of Precision (HDOP) and Geometric Dilution of Precision (GDOP) are used when measuring expected fix accuracy and, typically, a low HDOP number such as 02 appearing on the set is good news while a high number such as 07 is not. When a high number is revealed it is best to wait a little while and try again when the geometry has improved. What is called the status of satellites depends on position, signal strength and probable reliability,

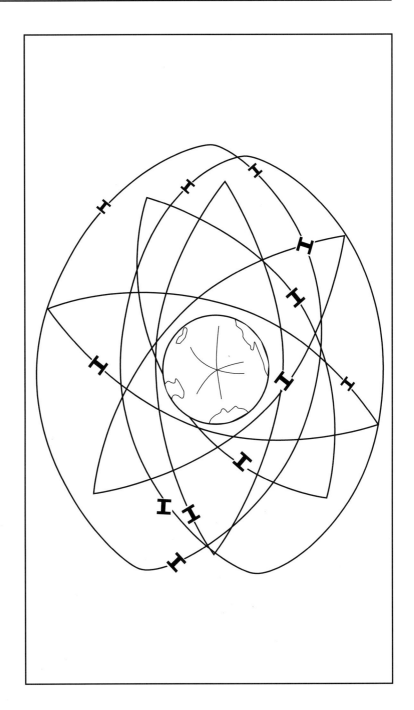

***Fig 1*** *Satellites providing a fix.*

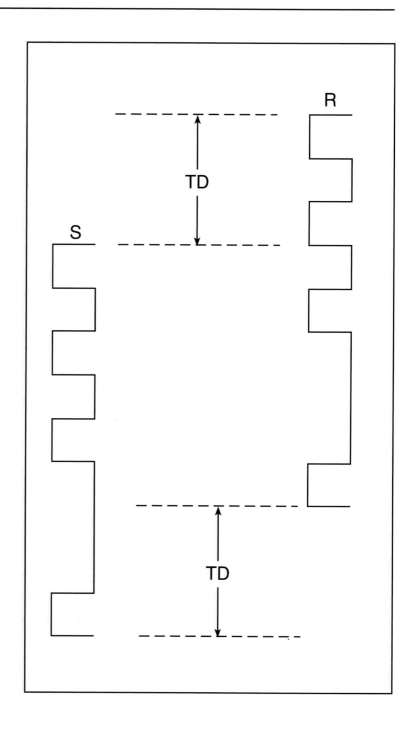

***Fig 2*** *Pseudo-random codes compared.*

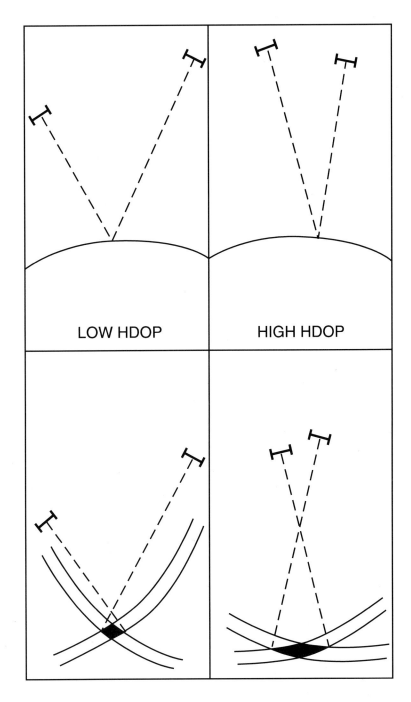

LOW HDOP          HIGH HDOP

***Fig 3*** *Good and bad satellite geometry, with the right-hand pair too close together and having larger range errors.*

and many sets show it coded as a number. The most important component is Signal Quality (SQ), and as sets are constructed to reveal it at the press of a button, it is as well to understand the nature of SQ at an early stage.

*SIGNAL
QUALITY*

Whereas Dilution of Precision (DOP) in its two forms is mostly about the placing of satellites, Signal Quality relates to the strength of signals from a particular satellite. The SQ number shown on the set is an indication of the carrier-to-noise or signal-to-noise ratio – the measurement of the quantitative relationship between the useful and non-useful parts of the signal. Readings in the 7–9 range mean that the signal is strong and useful, with 0–3 indicating that the set may lose lock and receive no decent signal. A GPS satellite whose signal fades is declared 'unhealthy' and its transmissions are coded so that the set ignores them. Some sets have a graphical representation of SQ by bar chart and others put a number alongside the satellite identification number. The question of satellite position and status is gone into in greater detail in Chapter 4.

*THE TWO
CODES AND
SELECTIVE
AVAILABILITY*

As was stated earlier, satellites transmit two kinds of data in two different codes. One tranche of data is called the Almanac and relates to such things as the satellite's time over the horizon, time of setting, angle of elevation and direction. The other is the Ephemeris, which covers the health of the satellite, its orbital parameters and, hence, the range to a terrestrial position. The information is put into one of two codes: the very accurate Protected (or Precision) Code, known as the P-Code, which is for military use, and the 'unprotected' Coarse (or Course) Acquisition Code – the C/A Code – which is what *we* get on our sets. The master station can, and does, degrade the accuracy of the civilian signal by means of variable adjustments so that for 95 per cent of the time the position given by your set is within a 100 metre radius of the true position, while the other 5 per cent is outside that circle of accuracy. Two euphemisms describe this deliberate degradation of the signal. The civilian user is said to be in receipt of the Standard

Positioning Service and the process of distortion is called Selective Availability. As you may imagine, both users of GPS and manufacturers of sets devote a great deal of time and ingenuity to circumventing the constraints of Selective Availability in order to get results similar to those provided by the P-Code. The modified civilian system that seeks to emulate military precision is called the Differential Global Positioning System (DGPS), and some of the sets we will be looking at can get the improved signal that gives a fix only five or ten metres in error. (See Figure 4 for the principle of DGPS.)

At the time of writing, the US Department of Defense has the means to switch off GPS altogether, and it has done so at least once in recent years. Seven satellites were switched off for seven hours during a public holiday in the United States in 1992 for reasons that may only be guessed at. As it happens, the Russian equivalent of GPS, called GLONASS (Global Navigation Satellite System), with 24 satellites aloft does *not* make use of Selective Availability and, in theory, could provide better coverage in Europe. It has been offered for general world-wide use without charge, but legal and control problems have yet to be ironed out. Eventually, we could see a Global Navigation Satellite System (GNSS) using Russian and American satellites that will be acceptable to the world's airlines and operating under the aegis of the United Nations, but at the moment a switch-off is always on the cards.

Mind you, yachtsmen are a little churlish in grumbling about a system that does not cost them anything, and the latest statement from the White House about the future of GPS is to the effect that Selective Availability will be phased out in ten years or so. This leaves users and the electronics industry in a bit of a dilemma. Is it worthwhile to spend research time and development money on a problem that may solve itself within a decade? Should users acquire the new technology when the passage of time will update the old technology anyway? It is probably best to hedge your bets; to know about the advantages of DGPS in the short term but play a waiting game until the future becomes clearer. The possibility of losing GPS transmissions through governmental action means

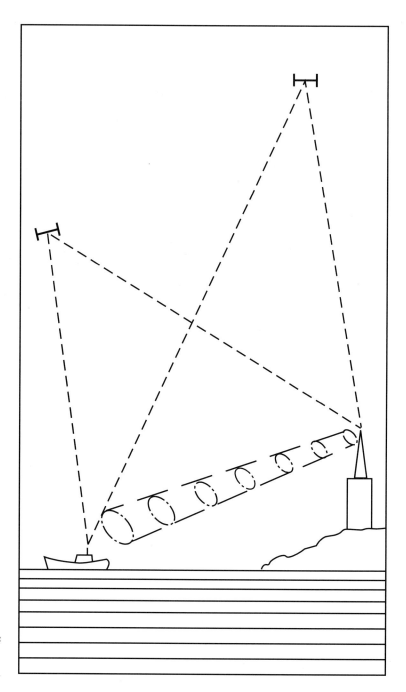

***Fig 4*** *The differ-ential beacon sends the corrected signal to the yacht.*

that a back-up electronic system is desirable. The operation of such a system is described in Chapter 8.

**EUROFIX**          Experiments at Delft University of Technology to combine signals from satellites and marine radio beacons with Loran-C transmissions have resulted in a system of position-fixing with an accuracy comparable to that achieved by Differential GPS. Eurofix has the advantage of using existing facilities to correct satellite position fixes because the location of marine radio beacons and Loran-C towers is known within feet. Receivers do not exist at the time of writing, but Eurofix seems to be an inexpensive solution to the problem of Selective Availability until it is phased out.

## 2 • GPS Sets and their Installation

There are two main types of receivers, fixed and hand-held, and the principal difference between them is that the former run on the boat's batteries or one specifically wired up for the purpose. In general, hand-helds run on shaver or torch batteries that require frequent renewal, but they are popular with small-craft owners because they take up hardly any space and can go home between trips. They are also cheaper and, at the time of writing, many cost under £100. It follows that the navigator who wants to link his GPS set to other electronic units such as a plotter, digitized chart, radar or autopilot must either choose a fixed set powered by 12-volt batteries or convert his hand-held to a fixed set by mounting it on a bracket and fitting an adaptor to receive 12-volt power. Attempts to run a number of units from shaver or torch batteries will result in a low power signal and a refusal of duty. There is another lithium battery in many sets that is soldered into position and difficult to replace at home. It powers the memory that stores data and will last up to five years. Replacement of the lithium battery should be carried out by the dealer who sold you the set, and it is a good idea to have this done every third year to ensure trouble-free operation.

*COMPATIBILITY* An American organization called the National Maritime Electronics Association (NMEA) sets world standards for the compatibility of electronic equipment. This takes the form of a numbered label so that, for example, if your GPS set has an NMEA 0183 label it will work with an autopilot bearing the same number. When buying a set be sure that it produces position in terms of latitude and longitude because there are some GPS sets designed for hill-walkers that give national grid coordinates or military grid references, although other sets convert readily enough from latitude and longitude to Ordnance Survey datum and can give either – see Chapter 10.

Take measurements beforehand to make sure your fixed

set will fit where it can be seen. Will it need a swing-out bracket? Is the power source close at hand? Remember that they are part radio receiver and part computer with both parts disliking vibration and damp. As a general rule, single channel units are cheaper and less accurate because they make averaging assumptions about speed and direction, while multi-channel receivers monitor more satellites but are bulkier and take up more space. Integration of compatible units is now catered for by manufacturers so that, for example, the Sea Talk combination from Autohelm has an electronic compass, GPS, radar, chart plotter, speed log, echo sounder, wind speed indicator and autopilot all available at the console or steering position.

A brief description of the sets referred to in this book follows. The first three are fixed, the remainder are hand-helds.

**RAYTHEON'S NAV 398** is a hybrid that receives signals from both types of GPS and Loran-C through the medium of up to three sensors mounted side by side. Figure 5 shows how a 'Y' cable assembly links two sensors to a receiver.

**MICROLOGIC'S ADMIRAL** is still selling at the time of writing and represents a bargain at the price, although it is some years old. It has an excellent display showing range and bearing to a waypoint.

**APELCO FISHFINDER/PLOTTER 560** is a depth-finder/ GPS unit that accepts its GPS input from a sensor. It has a simulator for 'dry runs' at home.

**MLR'S VALSAT SP** is French and a self-locator that needs no initialization. The screen has large letters and there is a 'help' function if you get confused with the keying.

**GARMIN GPS 12XL** is a new product and its twelve channels offer good performance in difficult conditions. It works well in a covered wheelhouse, and has a simulator.

**MICROLOGIC'S SPORTSMAN GPS** is one of the older sets, and one of the least expensive. It has a big screen and is wider than most hand-helds, making it a little awkward to grasp in rough conditions.

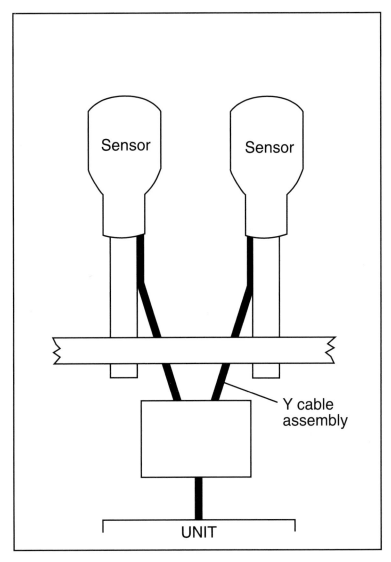

***Fig 5*** *'Y' cable assembly linking two sensors to a receiver.*

**EAGLE EXPLORER** was new in 1997 and the square cross-section fits well in the hand. The route-planning display is particularly clear and easy to follow.

The manufacturer's name will be left out hereafter and the sets referred to as:

| | |
|---|---|
| **NAV 398** | **ADMIRAL** |
| **FISHFINDER/PLOTTER 560** | **VALSAT SP** |
| **12XL** | **SPORTSMAN** |
| **EXPLORER** | |

*BATTERIES AND THE HAND-HELD SET*

It is important to keep a note of battery strength and how much time remains, and when a new one goes in to set the timer to zero. The procedure with the **Sportsman** to set the timer working is to key in ON/OFF MENU MENU N+W x 9 to get:

| | | |
|---|---|---|
| Light Time | 10s | |
| Shut-off Time | 10m | |
| Time on battery is | 00.09 | hr: min |

Touch CLR CLR CLR ENT and the timer will start to accumulate battery time used from zero. When nearly spent, you will get an alert message reading: BATTERY POWER IS LOW, PRESS CLR. There is now just ten minutes of battery life available and a second warning comes on automatically at five minutes. Ignore the latter and the set will shut down.

*ANTENNA AND SENSOR INSTALLA-TION*

The first principle to grasp is that a GPS set likes a clear expanse of sky but does not need the antenna set as high as possible. Signals may become unreliable close to tall structures, cranes, under trees, masts, sails, rigging and deckhouses, or inside buildings so that if you want to test your new fixed set on land it is best to go to a bare hill and either take an extra cable and plug it into the cigarette lighter socket in the car or take a 12-volt battery with you. At sea, the

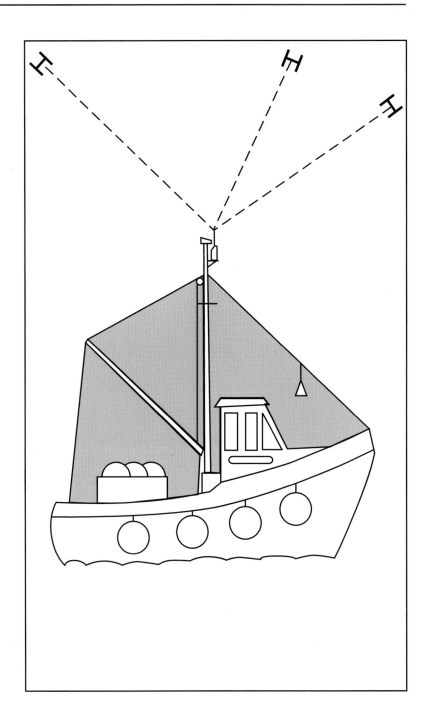

***Fig 6*** *Poor reception in shaded area.*

antenna for a sailing boat will work best from the pushpit or on a short pole right aft and at least a metre clear of other aerials and not in the path of a radar beam. Mast-top mounting should be avoided for pitch and roll will cause constant small changes to position figures and, in any case, the VHF aerial which is up there may create interference.

In motor craft, on the other hand, the antenna needs to be above all potentially 'shadowing' structures and, as in Figure 6, mast-top fitting is acceptable. Sensors work best when fitted high up on the flying-bridge. Similar factors come into play with hand-helds. If you can imagine two crewmen with hand-helds, one in the cockpit and shadowed by the mainsail and the other up by the mast and some six feet higher, the 'upstairs' set has the better chance of good signals. When a hand-held is wedged into a holder or fitted to a bracket with an aerial the set can be in any plane so long as the aerial is vertical. Some owners prefer it this way so that they can operate the keys with one hand and write down the position with the other. Others clove-hitch a piece of cord around their hand-helds so that they can be lashed to something solid in rough weather. They will work provided the additional antenna is upright.

*FITTING THE SET*

Fixed sets need to be accessible and protected from the weather, and in motor craft are commonly fitted to the console. Make sure there are no hidden wires or current-carrying instruments behind the selected site and try to leave seven inches of free space all around the set. This is hard to achieve in many small yachts but you should at least position the GPS set a minimum of 30 inches from a magnetic compass. Before screwing everything down, experiment by trying all the potential positions within reach of the power and antenna cables and check you've got the set properly wired up. With the **Admiral** the process goes something like this. Connect the antenna cable to a fitting at the back of the set marked ANTENNA INPUT. Turn off all other electrical and electronic units before connecting the power plug to a port marked 12 at the back of the set. Press the  ON/OFF  switch at the front of the set and the screen should illuminate and then shift to a

*Raytheon Marine Company GPS and Loran Sensors and Differential Beacon Receiver*

message saying ACQUIRING SATELLITES/DATA. Now switch off; the unit is going to work in the chosen position.

In sailing craft the set is often mounted at the navigator's work station on the bulkhead above the chart table, and a short-handed or racing crew may need to have an on-deck repeater to save constant trips up and down the companion-way to see what's going on. Some fixed sets may need grounding to ensure interference-free signals, and in a steel craft this is accomplished by running a wire strop from a but-terfly nut at the back of the set to the hull. A glassfibre yacht can get the same result by having a strop going from the set to the engine block or to a ground plate below the waterline. This ground wire 'draws' unwanted noise interference from the receiver and also provides some protection during electri-cal storms and lightning strikes. Finally, there is the antenna to consider. In a sailing boat this is often left out in the wind and rain for years on end, and such benign neglect is exactly the right policy. Whatever you do, *don't* paint it because if you do it may never work properly again. If you feel that the antenna should go home in the winter as part of a general clear-out or to test the set at home, remember that all it needs by way of attention is a dry wipe.

*ESSENTIAL*
*PRELIMINARIES*

People who are unfamiliar with machines worry about two aspects of their use: keying correctly and making mistakes. We'll deal with mistakes first. The set knows which are valid presses and which not so that with the **NAV 398**, for example, a valid press results in a single beep and a wrong one in three beeps. A CLR or a QUIT takes you back to position display or the selection menu on the screen. Some sets cancel everything that has gone before with a CLR and others need MODE or EXIT for the same purpose. The instruction manual should have this information. GPS sets have two types of keys. Hard keys have a single function, such as ENT, MARK, GOTO and CLR, while soft keys have more than one and are often adjacent to the screen so that when NAVIGATE or STEER appear, the nearest soft key is the one to press. Arrowed keys up-and-down ▲ or right-and-left ▶ enable the user to scroll between items in a list, such as waypoints. Finally, there is switch-off. To avoid accidental touches wiping out an entry, some sets require presses on two keys. The **Valsat SP**, for example, requires a press on the green ON/OFF button, which brings up the query 'do you want to switch off your GPS?' If you do, an ENTER is needed. Other units, and the **Explorer** is among their number, demand that the PWR or ON/OFF button is held down for three seconds or so, and a power-saving device on most sets switches them off if no keying takes place for a specified time.

*LATITUDE AND*
*LONGITUDE*
*FIGURES*

The presentation of latitude and longitude figures differs markedly from set to set, and the general rule in this book is that the printed page shows what each set displays. The sort of variations you will see for a latitude position include:

| | | |
|---|---|---|
| 50° 15.273 N | 50° 15.27 N | n 50° 15 273 |
| N 50° 15 273´ | N 50° 15.273´ | N 50° 15.27´ |
| | 50° 15 27 n | |

but they all convey the same information. When keying, the minute sign (´) and the dot between whole minutes and fractions of a minute can be ignored.

*THE CURE*
*FOR STARVED*
*AND SULKY*
*RECEIVERS,*
*AND*
*AVERAGING*

A 'starved' receiver is a single-channel unit, usually hand-held, which has been left on with no button pressed for some time. It continues to collect satellite data if the antenna is in the open air but the display has closed down to save battery power. If the set is in a locker or an oilskin jacket pocket it will take a couple of minutes to operate properly again. The answer, of course, is always turn off when not in use. A sulky receiver has poor status figures but should improve if left face up in one position for a period of time. Sometimes, as with the **Sportsman,** performance will improve with this treatment. This set has an averaging function if left on for up to 60 seconds because a number of readings are amalgamated to deliver a waypoint over time. This single fix procedure works with keying:

MENU  MENU  MENU  MENU   N+W  N+W  N+W  N+W

to disclose:

| | | |
|---|---|---|
| DLA    n | | 00 00.00 |
| DLO    w | | 000 00.00 |
| SINGLE FIX | | OFF |
| AVERAGE | | 15s |

CLR  CLR  CLR  brings the cursor onto the SINGLE FIX line and  ENT  and  CLR  put it on the AVERAGE line. Key in the desired time interval, say one minute, with  6  0  ENT . This averaged fix is stored as the LAST SAVED waypoint and, after a warning beep, the set switches off. It will next be displayed when  WPT  is pressed. Naturally, SINGLE FIX must be turned off afterwards otherwise all subsequent fixes will be in the same mode. The manufacturers say that a customer who used external power and left the set on for 24 hours achieved an accuracy figure of 15 metres – nearly as good as DGPS – but as the procedure entails using the set on a mooring or pontoon and not moving for a day, the exercise is academic rather than practical.

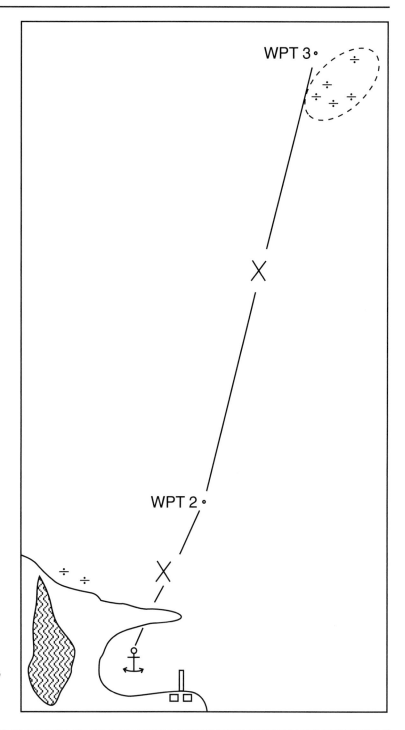

**Fig 7** Don't try to cross land or shave dangers too closely.

**LIMITATIONS ON USE**

A glance at Figure 7 on page 27 should convince you that there are two things a GPS user may not do. The craft at anchor in the bay cannot follow a course for waypoint 2 because of dry land in the way, and while the machine will supply the data, the navigator must have the good sense not to use it. At the top of Figure 7 a waypoint has been put close to a group of rocks. This is an unsafe practice because the track from waypoint 2 to waypoint 3 runs near to the danger. In this book, waypoints are put a mile or more away from reefs or headlands so that, for example, waypoint 7 off the Wolf Rock is at 49° 55′ N 005° 48′ W – over 1.5 miles south of the charted position. Putting the waypoint too close is foolish, and so is entering the position of a lighthouse or beacon tower as a waypoint. The better nautical almanacs put safe offshore waypoints in bold type, as in the case of 'OFFSHORE WAY-POINT OFF BLANKENBERGE 51° 19′.5 N, 3° 06′.0 E.' Waypoint listings should be checked on the chart to allow the proper clearance and ensure there is no intervening land. There are enough GPS-assisted strandings on record to emphasize the importance of these precautions and at the start of a trip the machine should not be brought into use until open water is reached. Similarly, it makes no sense to rely wholly on the proximity alarm to give notice that the rock, buoy or beacon aimed for is right under the bow when a little forward planning will bring it comfortably and safely abeam. The rule is: be close enough to identify but not so close as to endanger the ship.

The first television sets required a period of time to warm up after being switched on, and some unprepared GPS sets may take time to acquire satellites and provide a position fix from a cold start. However, if the GPS set is told roughly where it is on the surface of the earth, it should supply a fix in a minute or so. This first start or initialization process entails entering the approximate latitude and longitude of present position, the height of the antenna or sensor above sea level (not so important at sea but may be needed if you are prac-tising at home), date and time. This procedure must be followed with a new set or when present location is over 100 miles from where the set was last used. If, of course, the set is going to be used at the same location as when it went off last season, it should re-acquire signals without initialization. You will soon know if things are not right. If a flashing display persists for some minutes, this is a sure sign that the start-up routine must be followed. This important first step is illus-trated by three examples.

*INITIALIZING THE FISHFINDER/ PLOTTER 560*

Begin with PWR ► NAVIGATION MENU ► NAV STATUS ► GPS ► top soft key and a GPS STATUS display comes up on the screen. At the top is an estimated position which may be nothing like the real one, so key in an approximate latitude and longitude for where you are now. The entry is:

5  1  2  4  0  0  ►  ►  ENTER

0  0  1  3  2  1  7  ►  ENTER

Put in antenna or sensor height with an ENTER , if you wish. The date goes in backwards with the year first, then the month, then the day:

9 7 0 4 0 8 ▶ ENTER

while time goes in as a four-figure number:

1 6 2 6 ▶ ENTER

The GPS STATUS page now reveals itself:

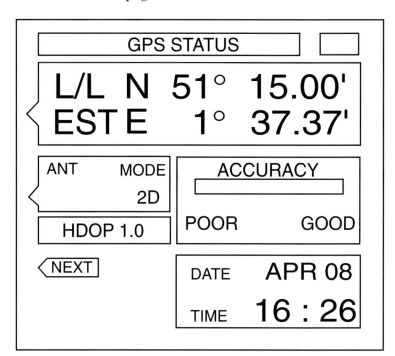

*Fig 8* *The GPS Status Page after initialization.*

Is anything wrong? Yes, the estimated longitude is an easterly figure and should be a westerly one. Touch the top ▶ and re-key the latitude plus ▶ ENTER ▶ ENTER . Key in the longitude numbers and add ▶ ENTER ▶ E W ▶ ENTER . One more ▶ ENTER gets you back to antenna height and date and time. A further press of ▶ ENTER ▶ ENTER restores the GPS STATUS page, with all now correct.

The information on it reads – from the top – your present position, an indication of how many satellites the set is receiving signals from and a low HDOP number showing that fix accuracy is excellent. The date and time are as you entered them. If the accuracy had been doubtful it would have shown up on the ACCURACY scale between POOR and GOOD. No antenna height was given in this example so there is a blank below ANT. First start should only be required once a season if the unit is in regular use because with many sets all the waypoints and other data you have put in will be wiped out or changed with first start procedure. Naturally, if you move to a new sea area and want to cancel data relating to the old one a first start does the deed.

*FIRST START –*
*ADMIRAL*

Press the   ON/OFF   key for one second and then go to MENU  MENU  and, by repeated scrolling with the + or − buttons, bring up FIRST START PROCEDURE.

An   ENT   now produces detailed instructions and the display changes to HOLD CLR DOWN FOR 10 SEC. This brings up the PROCEDURE block inviting data insertion and starting with the time zone. In this case the set is in Florida where the time zone is +5 hours on Greenwich and you need to touch  + 5  followed by local time, date and approximate latitude and longitude as indicated by a flashing cursor. This set has the modern trendy practice of giving thousandths of a minute, so the approximate reading after keying is:

2 4 0 0 0 0 0  ENT

0 8 0 0 0 0 0  ENT

and you must imagine a decimal point between the two zeroes representing minutes and the three standing for thousandths of a minute.

Altitude is the next item. The antenna on the pushpit is six feet above water level so that  6 ENT  is needed. The start-up is completed with a READY on a soft key and the next touch of  POS  should give latitude and longitude after a short interval. Navigators are renowned doubting Thomases and if you want to find out if this start-up has 'taken', just touch the right-hand soft key under the screen that gives TIME.

The page should then look like this:

| Time Zone/Day Light | |
|---|---|
| EASTERN STANDARD | +5 hrs |
| LOCAL TIME<br>16:52:53 | Monday<br>20<br>October 1997 |
| UTC/GMT<br>21:52:53 | |

The letters UTC at bottom left stand for Universal Time Coordinated, which is an ultra-accurate version of GMT (Greenwich Mean Time).

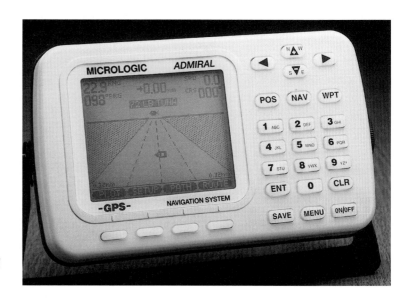

*Micrologic Admiral GPS set.*

**INITIALIZATION WITH THE SPORTSMAN**  Touch ON/OFF and hold CLR down for six seconds until an identification message appears and any test data has gone off the screen. Press NAV NAV NAV NAV and a grid shows up reading:

```
Lat n    00°00′.000

Lon w   00°00′.000

Accuracy    9999 ft

Altitude        0ft
```

Now enter the approximate latitude and longitude of your present location with:

CLR   5   1   ENT   and   0   0   1   ENT

ignoring everything except whole degrees. Height of the antenna goes in next as:

CLR   2   0   0   ENT

because you are well inland and 200 feet above sea level. The next step is to make sufficient  MENU  presses to get the time zone. The set may show:

```
EASTERN STANDARD            +5

TIME                    11:39:07

MON OCT              27  1997

UTC/GMT                16:39:07
```

and the bottom two lines need no correction. However, we are in the wrong time zone for the UK, and local time is not five hours ahead of UTC/GMT. Touch  CLR  S-E  several times to bring the reading to correspond to UTC/GMT. A touch on  NAV  gives position, accuracy and altitude as follows.

```
LAT            n 51° 15′ 298

LON          w 001° 37′ 393

ACCURACY            156 ft

ALTITUDE            200 ft
```

*SETS THAT NEED NO FIRST START – THE VALSAT SP, THE EXPLORER AND THE NAV 398*

The hand-held French set takes between one and three minutes to acquire satellites and the procedure involves switching on to reveal a logo and a welcoming message. A first  PAGE  shows what satellites are available and a second  PAGE  gives the latitude and longitude as:

51° N 15.302          001° W 37.344

together with time, date and altitude. The **Explorer** can be initialized or given a cold start and the procedure for the latter is to key  PWR  navigational warning  EXIT  and watch for the flashing display to cease and the position to show up. It takes about two minutes – the same time as the manual initialization.  WPT   WPT  saves it in the memory by number. The **NAV 398** has a NOW TESTING beginning and, when complete, the screen shows:

| | |
|---|---|
| ROM | OK |
| RAM | OK |
| SENSOR | OK |

followed by a signal grid which will be analysed in the next chapter. If NG appears in place of OK, as with SENSOR NG, it is time to check connections. The next reading is the position, which is:

N   51° 15 32

W 001° 37 40

(the location of the set in my back garden in central southern England). Note that there are very slight differences in the position given by four of the sets – some fractions of a minute. This is not unusual, particularly when altitude has not been put in, and different readings are often recorded from sets at the bow and the stern of vessels. Remember that Selective Availability only confers accuracy within 100 metres for 95 per cent of the time, so that 200 metres from side to side of your circle of position is the expected margin of error and should always be taken into account when navigating in congested waters. (See Figure 17, the probability ellipse.)

*THE 12XL HAS TWO FIRST START PROCEDURES*

The first is based on geography and national boundaries, with the names of countries put in to initialize the **12XL**. After ON WELCOME and the satellite-searching display, an ENTER superimposes a block on the page reading:

> CHOOSE INIT
>
> METHOD
>
> I. SELECT
>    COUNTRY
>    FROM LIST
> 2. AUTOLOCATE
> 3. NO RE-INIT
>    (CONTINUE
>    SEARCHING)

Usually, COUNTRY is highlighted at this point, but if not, a scroll up makes it so and an ENTER gives the first page, headed Afghanistan. Continue with ▼ until you reach the page headed Turks and Caicos, which has USA-AK high-lighted at the bottom. If your home port is Pwllheli in North Wales, scroll up once ▲ to arrive at UK-Wales and ENTER it. With a Scottish base go up another ▲ to UK-Scotland and ENTER it. Two more ▲ ▲ takes you to UK-England and if that is where your yacht is ENTER it. AUTOLOCATE is for idle navigators, but it may take five minutes before anything meaningful shows up. The NO RE-INIT facility is used when a set has already been initialized but the antenna is shaded and the unit is still slowly collecting satellite information.

*EAST OF GREENWICH, SOUTH OF THE EQUATOR*

Sets usually reach their users with north latitude and west longitude appearing on the display. If your sailing area is east of the Greenwich meridian or south of the equator, a manual correction is required. The **Admiral** and the **Sportsman** have an S-E key for the alteration and when cruising between Newhaven and Brighton on the English side of the Channel, or Le Havre and Ouistreham on the French coast, you must be aware that neglecting the change creates east/west error. The **NAV 398** embodies this change with the SIGNAL STATUS page that appears soon after switch-on. An EST soft key reveals the estimated position and an ENTER brings up a soft key arrow pointing to N/S and another ENTER the E/W soft key. Mediterranean sailors must be prepared to change the sign quite often when voyaging up and down Spain's east coast, and north/south error is a common operating mistake when going from the west coast of North America to Tahiti. Fortunately, the very magnitude of the error soon tells the navigator that he has gone wrong.

*NO USEFUL SIGNAL*

The most disconcerting thing that can happen after initialization is to get a meaningless response. Here are two such examples. The POS key on an **Admiral** set is touched and after a short delay the screen shows SATS REC'D 0/5 and ACC 9999 feet. This means that although five satellites are theoretically available none are being received, while the 9999 feet figure suggests that a fix cannot be computed. The Sky Plot that shows on the screen after POS usually gives the azimuth (direction) of each satellite, so what has gone wrong? There are two possibilities. If you have mis-keyed the latitude and longitude figures, the start-up may not have 'taken' and the initialization procedure needs to be done again. Second, the position of the antenna may not be right. Perhaps it is not vertical or it may be in the 'shadow' of something substantial so that signals are blocked, or it could be improperly connected. The **Valsat SP** has a useful and informative display for the occasion, which looks like this:

```
P        POSITION        4
         WARNING
         NO POSN FIX
         LAST POSITION
         50° 15.273 N
         003° 06.214 W
         002 m
         15:44:14
         11/11/97
```

with the last fix shown to help the navigator see where he was a while ago. With a hand-held set that refuses duty, check its battery strength and move it a few feet before trying again. See Chapter 10 for a checklist of faults.

*TRUE OR MAGNETIC NORTH?*

Most GPS sets leave the factory programmed to give courses and bearings in relation to magnetic north and take account of changes in variation automatically. The mode is termed Auto Mag. If a navigator wants to use true courses and bearings to match the figures given by a fluxgate compass, he must make a manual correction. The **12XL** has an Auto Mag default setting and to make the change to true, start with ON WELCOME and the satellite status display followed by PAGE PAGE PAGE PAGE PAGE PAGE PAGE . Scroll down ▼ to NAVIGATION and ENTER it. NAV SETUP appears and at the foot of the page is HEADING Auto Mag EOO3. Scroll down again with ▼ and use an ENTER to highlight the 'A' in Auto Mag. Three more touches on ▼ show True and it may be ENTER ed to confirm the change.

# 4 • *Status and Position*

Just as people want to know what the weather is going to be like today or tomorrow, so yachtsmen seek to establish if their GPS sets are going to give good results. We will now look at four examples of signal status information from two hand-held sets and two fixed sets.

*STATUS WITH THE 12XL*

After ON and WELCOME, a SEARCHING EPE grid appears. This soon changes to ACQUIRING EPE. In what follows, the outer circle represents the horizon and the inner 45° above the horizontal, with the 'best' satellites in or close to the latter.

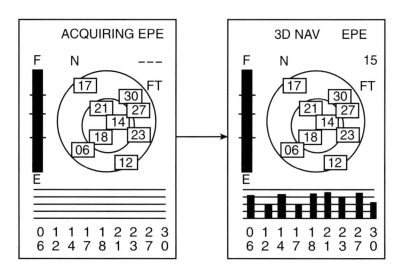

At the foot of the right-hand drawing the signal strength is shown by bars, and satellites 21, 14, 18 and 27 appear to be giving a good 3D fix. The position page comes up next and gives track, speed, trip distance, altitude, latitude and longitude and time. To put the position in the memory as a waypoint, touch MARK and then name it. The bar with an

F and an E at each end to the left of the circular sky view shows battery level – this one is giving full power.

*SIGNAL*
*STATUS  WITH*
*THE NAV 398*

The readout of signal status again comes immediately before the position is displayed, and the interpretation of the top half of the display goes like this:

| GPS SIGNAL STATUS | | | | | | | | |
|---|---|---|---|---|---|---|---|---|
| (Satellite identification numbers) | 06 | 28 | 25 | 05 | 24 | 29 | 01 | 22 |
| (Azimuth angle)  A | S | S | W | E | NE | NW | SW | W |
| (Elevation above horizon)  E | 79 | 76 | 57 | 25 | 24 | 21 | 14 | 11 |
| (Signal level)  L | 46 | 00 | 43 | 40 | 45 | 00 | 35 | 38 |
| | | | | | | | | HDOP 01.0 |

Blocked satellite numbers in the top line have locked-on. When there are four or more, this display vanishes and a position is shown. Signal status can also be found at times other than switch-on with a MENU and GL/O . Each reading is a snapshot of status and if the display is left on, some satellites will become more useful and others will fade away. In practice, you can leave the set to get on with it after switch-on because it cannot display a position until the geometry is right. In the next example, the information comes piecemeal and there is a useful indication of the accuracy of the fix.

*STATUS*
*WITH THE*
*HAND-HELD*
*SPORTSMAN*

This is a simpler layout and line four is the first to appear, so the screen shows:

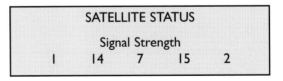

| SATELLITE STATUS | | | | |
|---|---|---|---|---|
| Signal Strength | | | | |
| 1 | 14 | 7 | 15 | 2 |

with these five being the numbers of useful satellites. As time goes on, the third line begins to fill with starred numbers representing the signal strength. The scale runs from 1 to 9 with anything over 7 being first-rate but lower figures being more and more suspect (under 3 is quite useless). The display now shows:

| SATELLITE STATUS | | | | |
|:---:|:---:|:---:|:---:|:---:|
| Signal Strength | | | | |
| 7 | 5 | 5 | 7 | 6 |
| I | 14 | 7 | 15 | 2 |

When the data accumulation is complete, it changes to:

| LAT | n 51° 15.273 |
|---|---|
| LON | w 001° 37.377 |
| ACCURACY | 699 ft |
| ALTITUDE | 200 ft |

What sort of fix is it? Only moderate because of the high accuracy figure. One of, say, 160 feet would be acceptable. Above 2,500 feet the machine comes up with POSITION, SPEED NOT ACCURATE to show that the fix is wholly unreliable.

***STATUS WITH THE GPS SENSOR 182X AND THE FISHFINDER/ PLOTTER 560***

Here we can follow on from the initialization process described in Chapter 3 and Figure 8. ▶ NEXT reveals the GPS status page in Figure 9. The window on the left gives data in relation to satellite 22, which is at the lower limb of the oval on the right. It is boxed, which means it is of some value, but how good is it? The HDOP is fine and the signal strength is adequate. The angle is the critical figure. If it is less than 15°, distrust it. H25 at top left of the oval is unboxed, a sure sign that it is of little use, and this can be confirmed by scrolling through using the top soft key. It has an angle of 11° above the horizon and the signal strength is weak. Four satellites are giving a 3D fix and by touching  0  MODE  ▶  NAV  ▶  NAV  the position will show up.

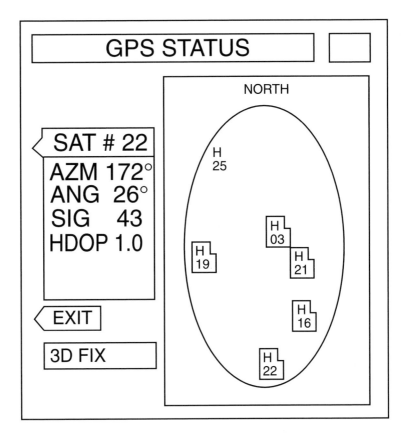

***Fig 9*** *How are the status figures performing today?*

**USE OF STATUS DATA**     Provided that the set is giving good fixes on demand, most users will not be greatly concerned about status, but there are occasions when knowledge of elevation and azimuth (or bearing) shapes actions. In Figure 10 a yacht has three satellites potentially in view but the one on the left is masked by high land and the yacht must move away from that land to get a signal. Similarly, in Figure 11, although three satellites *should* be available, two of them are at low angles and blocked on that particular bearing by island peaks. A move of a mile or so to the south-east or north-east, or a wait of three minutes, will improve reception on slightly different azimuths. Finally, there is the matter of unhealthy satellites. A scroll through the list may show that a particular satellite is TEMP OFF or OFF, as is sometimes the case.

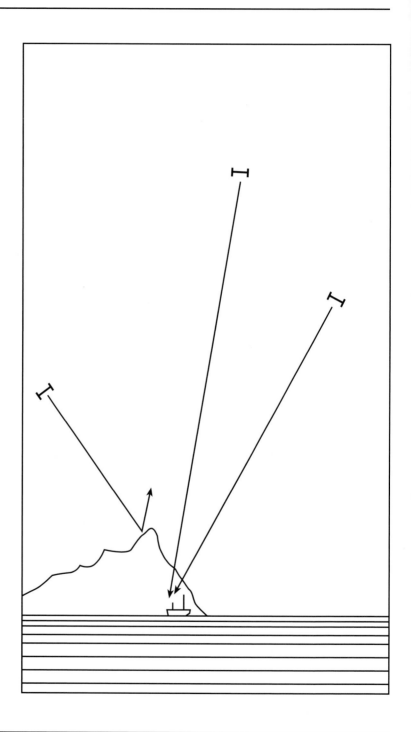

***Fig 10*** *Mask angle from high land.*

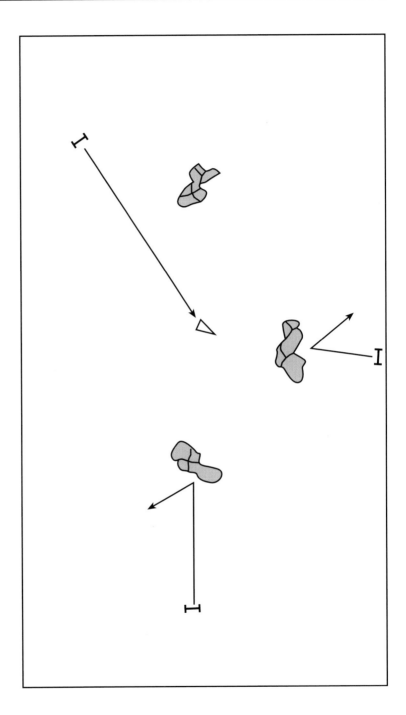

**Fig 11** *Masking from islands.*

*FORECASTS*    Some sets allow you to check future status. This is useful
when satellites have been declared unhealthy for one reason
or another. The **Admiral** runs a check after POS when the
Sky Plot appears and several presses of GPS reveals a graph
of accuracy predictions for 24 hours. With this set you can
also enter a future date for a long-term forecast. The screen
has, in its lower half, a display giving the number of satellites,
the mask angle and the times when each one is available for
a fix. The **Sportsman** has a similar facility and the satellite
schedule is triggered by MENU MENU MENU MENU,
bringing up:

> TO SEE SATELLITE
>
> SCHEDULE PRESS +
>
> ENTER DATE/MASK
>
> ANGLE TO COMPUTE

A touch on N+W precedes entry of the date and a mask
angle of 15° is in the memory and registers unless you want
to change it. A CLR gives the opportunity to enter the date
so that the forecast appears after using the + key. The forecast comes in six-hour periods with a satellite availability
number for each fifteen minutes. Another + and the next six-
hour forecast comes up. Each six-hour page looks like this,
with between four and six satellites available all the time:

| N+W | TIME | NUMBER OF SATELLITES | |
|---|---|---|---|
| | 00  01 | 4555 | 5544 |
| | 02  03 | 5666 | 5544 |
| | 04  05 | 5666 | 6666 |

*PLOTTING*      Having obtained a position with your GPS set, and being
*THE POSITION*  reasonably satisfied with its accuracy, what comes next? If
you are lucky enough to have a linked chart plotter, a small

*Fig 12* Plotting a fix.

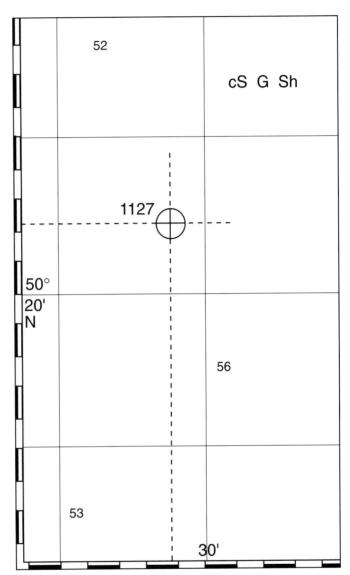

flashing cursor shows present position on a miniaturised chart and the latitude and longitude appears at the edge of the screen. However, most small boat owners using a hand-held set are not in this fortunate position and will be navigating with paper charts.

Imagine that your craft is in the English Channel south of Portland Bill and the position is:

N 50° 22.328
W 002° 31.245

The navigator starts by finding the mark on the side scale for 50° and then counts up the scale to make a pencil tick at about 22.3 minutes above it. He then lays a parallel ruler on the 50° line of latitude and moves the ruler upwards, taking care not to skew it, and, when the upper edge touches the pencil mark, draws in the line of latitude – the horizontal dotted line in Figure 12. Similarly, using the bottom scale, he puts in a mark for just over 31 minutes to the left of the 30 minute line of longitude and draws in a vertical line as in Figure 12. Where the lines intersect is the fix and the convention is that it be circled and the time entered alongside. The process is even easier when using a Breton plotter. These useful instruments have a median line at a right angle to the edges. By sliding the plotter up or along the side or foot of the chart until the median line is on the pencil mark, put in another mark at the other end of the median line. Using a straight-edged ruler, draw a line between the two marks, extending it if necessary to wherever it is needed on the chart. A second line created in the same way gives an intersection and a fix. This GPS-provided information can be used to set a course or update a plot, although experienced users will pass these tasks to the machine in a manner to be described later.

## 5 • Going Places

Waypoints are positions you want to get to, or return to. Because repeatable accuracy is the cornerstone of GPS operation, it is vital that they be noted and stored in the machine's memory. Waypoints go in the memory as latitude and longitude positions, and can also be named. The operator takes them from the chart or an almanac and can also make present position a waypoint. This last is the easiest way of recording and storing them, and two examples follow.

*STORING PRESENT POSITION AS A WAYPOINT WITH THE VALSAT SP*

Imagine that your yacht has left Deauville and is about a mile offshore and clear of all dangers. You need a waypoint to use as a departure mark for future calculations. The first keying sequence is to change the set from the default LEVEL 1 mode to LEVEL 2. After switch-on, the 1-2-3 logo appears and then the WELCOME page. Use ▶ to change GUIDE? to PERSONAL? at the foot of the display and confirm with an ENTER. Scroll across with ▶ to get to LEVEL and ENTER once more. LEVEL 2 is now highlighted and a touch on MARK brings up:

```
MARK

WPT:WPT 016

LAT: N 49°.23.410

LON: E 000°.03.248

COMMENT

SAVE?
```

When VALID appears on the menu bar, a last ENTER puts this waypoint into the memory.

*STORING A WAYPOINT WITH THE NAV 398*

It is a useful exercise to record the waypoint of where you live. After the usual preliminaries, the **NAV 398** comes up with:

> N   51° 15.32′
> W 001° 37.42′

and bottom right is GPS 2D indicating a reasonable fix.

A touch on   WPT 4   gives access to the memory and the invitation to ENTER NEW WAYPOINT ▶ . Touching the soft key to the right of the arrow brings up the next vacant number – 003 – and an   ENTER   discloses:

> 003 STORE WAYPOINT BY LAT/LON

suggesting the insertion of the latitude and longitude. Touch:

> 5   1   1   5   3   2   ENTER
>
> 0   0   1   3   7   4   2   ENTER

and the waypoint is stored. If you make a mistake, a   CLEAR   gives a second chance. Check that the new entry is in with   CLEAR   WPT 4   and the soft key GOTO WPT LIST. This shows that waypoint 3 is indeed at the right latitude and longitude. A   CLEAR   CLEAR   gives the exit back to POS on the screen. The instant waypoint is a one-off opportunity dependent on where you are at the time, but when planning a voyage it is often necessary to select one from the chart and record it by number, name and latitude and longitude.

*CREATING AND NAMING A WAYPOINT WITH THE SPORTSMAN*

Waypoints may be recorded by number or name, or both. With this set, present position is always waypoint zero. The first destination waypoint is going to be south and west of the Nab Tower to the east of the Isle of Wight. The selected position is N 50° 37′.00 000   W 001° 02′.00 000. Start by touching   WPT   and the screen reveals:

|  |  |
|---|---|
| WPT I | – – – – – – – |
| 3052 nm | 183 |
| LAT | N      00 00.000 |
| LON | W    000 00.000 |

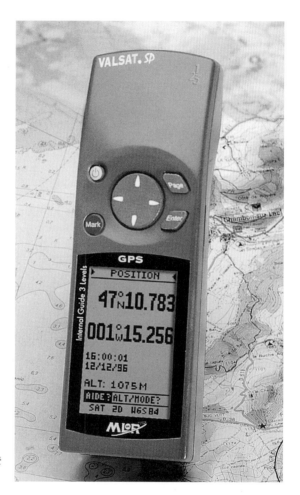

*The MLR Valsat
SP set.*

Waypoint 1 is 'empty' and available, while the seven dashes
to the right are for the name. The figures come first. Press
CLR until zeroes appear in place of 1 and then touch
1 ENT . Put in the latitude and longitude:

5   0   3   7   0   0   0   ENT

0   0   1   0   2   0   0   0   ENT

and waypoint 1 is in the memory. To name it press CLR until
a string of small letter 'a's appear top right in place of the

dashes. We want to call this waypoint NAB, so key:

| | | | |
|---|---|---|---|
| 5MNO | 5MNO | N+W | (for the letter 'N') |
| 1ABC | | N+W | (for the letter 'A') |
| 1ABC | 1ABC | N+W | (for the letter 'B') |

and confirm with  ENT . To check that the machine has got it right, key  WPT   WPT  so that the top line of the next display shows that WPT 1 is the same thing as NAB and below comes the date, time, accuracy estimate and altitude.

*STORING AND NAMING A NUMBER OF WAYPOINTS*

In Chapter 3 the **Fishfinder/Plotter 560** was initialized and the first position noted. It was not stored, but to simplify matters we will treat the first stored and named waypoint as waypoint 2. To enter this one, and five others, start with PWR ▶ NAVIGATION MENU ▶ WAYPOINT LIST/ROUTE ▶ LIST so that the next vacancy is 002. Scroll ▶ ENTER ▶ and the DATA soft key ▶ L/L. Key in the numbers for a waypoint south of St Catherine's Point at the southern extremity of the Isle of Wight:

| 5 | 0 | 3 | 3 | 0 | 0 | ▶ | ENTER |
|---|---|---|---|---|---|---|---|

| 0 | 0 | 1 | 1 | 7 | 0 | 0 | ▶ | ENTER |
|---|---|---|---|---|---|---|---|---|

Touch ▶ NAME and use the arrows at the foot of the display to pick out the letters in turn. The next entry reads C ▶ ADD A ▶ ADD P ▶ ADD 0 ▶ ADD and finish with ▶ ENTER . The full entry shows up as:

002  CAPO
N 50° 33.00′
W  1° 17.00′

The next five waypoints off Portland Bill, Start Point, Falmouth, the Lizard and Wolf Rock can go in in the same way. The memory then holds them as:

003    BILL
N 50° 25.00′
W  2° 27.00′

004    STAR
N 50° 10.00´
W  3° 45.00´

005 FALMO
N 50° 06.05´
W  4° 56.00´

006        LIZ
N 49° 56.00´
W  5° 12.00´

007   WOLF
N 49° 55.00´
W  5° 18.00´

Their use in making a route is dealt with in the next chapter.

*A ONE-LEG VOYAGE WITH THE NAV 398*

These journeys between one waypoint and another are the simplest form of a route. Here we will make the trip from HOME to CAPO. It does not matter that this is mostly over land because, as explained at the end of Chapter 2, the set cannot discriminate between travel over sea or land. The **NAV 398** found HOME to be at N 51° 15.32´, W 001° 37.42´ and CAPO was a navigator's selection at N 50° 33.00´, W 001° 17.00´. The memory already has HOME so to put in CAPO, key  WPT 4  to bring up ENTER NEW WPT? The ▶ and a touch on the soft key disclose the next vacant number and the invitation to store it by latitude and longitude. The soft key prompts entry and the figures go in as:

5   0   3   3   0   0   ENTER

0   0   1   1   7   0   0   ENTER   ENTER

When GOTO WPT LIST follows, another touch on the soft key confirms that the new waypoint is indeed at:

N    50° 33.00´
W   001° 17.00´

To get from HOME to WPT 2, key  GOTO 7  0  0  2  ENTER and top left in the display appears BRG 168° and DTG 44.2 nm

– meaning that the direction of travel is 168° and the distance to go is 44.2 nautical miles.

*A CHILLY ONE-LEG TRIP TO THE QUEEN CHARLOTTE ISLANDS WITH THE EXPLORER*

This time we are on the Pacific coast of Canada and sailing from Griffith Harbour on Banks Island to Skidegate Inlet on the eastern side of the Queen Charlotte Islands across the foggy Hecate Strait. The departure waypoint is at:

> N   53° 36.22´
> W 130° 36.10´

and has been entered in the **Explorer**'s memory as waypoint 9. The arrival waypoint is at:

> N   53° 16.28´
> W 131° 50.25´

and is waypoint 8. The distance is about 50 nm and after leaving Benilla Island to port it is open sea all the way. This is a reverse-order leg so that RUN REVERSE has to show on the ROUTES page in place of RUN FORWARD.

Begin with  PWR  navigational warning  EXIT  MENU  and highlight PLAN/EDIT ROUTES. A ▶ and a route number appears. Go ▼ to EDIT NAME and ▶ it. Use ▲ and ▼ to spell out CADA – the name for this mini-route – and  ENT  it. An  EXIT  takes you back to the route page and a ▲ to EDIT ROUTE. A ▶ reveals the waypoint list and ▶ ▶ the ADD WPTS page. The waypoint numbers go in as 8 ▼ ADD WPT ▶ ▶ and 9  ADD WPT ▶. At the foot of the page appears the courseline – 250° – and the distance is 48.45 nm.

*A ONE-LEG VOYAGE TO THE BAHAMAS*

On the other side of the continent, and in much warmer waters, let us run through a trip from the entrance to Biscayne Bay near Miami to Gun Key in the Bahamas, from:

N 25° 39.540´ W 080° 02.710´ to N 25° 33.410´ W 079° 18.890´.

We'll name them as EGGS and BACON respectively.

Start with the waypoint entries, which go in like this when using the **Sportsman**: ON/OFF advertising logo

SATELLITE STATUS. Key  WPT  CLR  to reveal a flashing cursor for the next waypoint number. It is going to be way-point 12 so the entry is  1  2  ENT .  CLR  CLR  precedes the insertion of the latitude and longitude, thus:

|  | 2 | 5 | 3 | 9 | 5 | 4 | 0 | ENT |
|---|---|---|---|---|---|---|---|---|
| CLR | 0 | 8 | 0 | 0 | 7 | 7 | 1 | 0 | ENT |

with  CLR  CLR  bringing up a flashing 'a' for name inser-tion. Key:

2DEF  2DEF  N+W  3GHI  N+W  3GHI  N+W  7STU  ENT

and EGGS appears on the screen.

Similarly,  WPT  1  3  ENT  CLR  CLR  followed by:

|  | 2 | 5 | 3 | 3 | 4 | 1 | 0 | ENT |
|---|---|---|---|---|---|---|---|---|
| CLR | 0 | 7 | 9 | 1 | 8 | 8 | 9 | 0 | ENT |

and  CLR  CLR  puts in waypoint 13. To name BACON touch:

1ABC  1ABC  N+W  1ABC  N+W  1ABC  1ABC  1ABC  N+W

5MNO  5MNO  5MNO  N+W  5MNO  5MNO  N+W  ENT

and the top line reads WPT 13 BACON.

To get from EGGS to BACON touch  ROUTE  and bring up a display headed FR – TO. Touch  CLR  and then put in the TO waypoint first as  1  3  ENT  CLR  and the FROM waypoint as  1  2  ENT . The page now reads:

| FR | 12 → | TO | 13 |
|---|---|---|---|
| EGGS | → | | BACON |
| 39.98 nm | | | 103° |
| ROUTE (number) | | | OFF |

*LONGER*
*ONE-LEG*
*VOYAGES*

Lengthy courselines need intermediate reference points and it is sound practice to put bars across the courseline at regular intervals to give an estimated position for, say, every two hours. With an average speed under sail of five knots, that calls for a bar every ten miles. The voyage from waypoint 1 (NAB) to waypoint 16 off Deauville necessitates eight such bars so that if the set gives up the ghost there is a marker, or dead reckoning position, to work from. If you want to use your GPS set to its full potential, enter these reference markers as waypoints along a route – for that is what this one-leg trip has now turned into. An additional bonus is that the waypoints provide an opportunity to check the accuracy of the log over ten miles, so, if, as is often the case under sail, the log is under-registering, the percentage of error can be noted. Five per cent error is common with slow-moving craft and it is good to have this kind of information for future trips.

*DELETING A*
*WAYPOINT*

Having toiled over the keys to acquire waypoints it seems ironic that the time will come when we have to get rid of some of  them to make room for more. The **Valsat SP** holds 600 in the memory, but when one or more is redundant the keying to dispose of a waypoint from, say, a sea area you are unlikely to visit again goes like this:

1-2-3 logo WELCOME PAGE PAGE PAGE PAGE PAGE PAGE

which brings up the GO TO WPT heading. A ▶ discloses EDI in the menu bar;   ENTER   it. EDIT WPT comes next and ▼ ▼ gets you to DELETE, which calls for an  ENTER . The WPT LIST has an invitation to:

SELECT THE WPT TO BE DELETED

and WPT 001 is highlighted. If this is to go, touch ENTER ENTER . Otherwise, scroll through to find the candidate(s) for oblivion and  ENTER   ENTER  it or them. Waypoints deleted in this way can always go back in again if you find later that the execution was premature.

It often happens that a set arrives from the dealer with a waypoint in the memory from half-way round the world

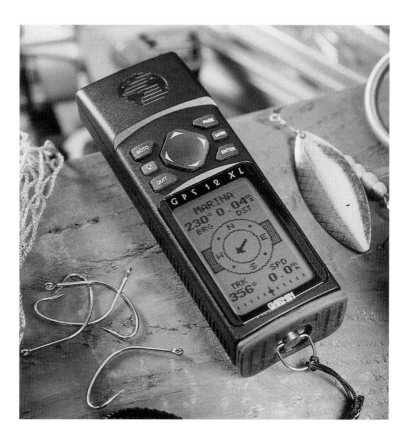

*Garmin's 12 XL.*

where it was tested and you have to eliminate it straight away. The procedure with the **12XL** starts with ON , the WELCOME page and satellite status display and you have to key PAGE x 7 for the Menu. Scroll ▲ or ▼ for WAYPOINT and ENTER it. Then scroll ▼ and ◄ to get to DELETE. ENTER that and ◄ to confirm YES, finishing with a final ENTER . The **Explorer's** route to deleting a waypoint begins with PWR navigational warning EXIT WPT . Scroll ▼ to OPTIONS and ► it. Scroll ▼ again to DELETE WPT and ►. A message appears saying 'ARE YOU SURE YOU WANT TO DELETE WPT NUMBER 1?' and YES and NO boxes are available for your decision. Press ► to remove it and ◄ to exit without removing the waypoint from the memory.

# 6 • The Waypoint Directory: Making and Using a Route

**WAYPOINT DIRECTORY**

Some old-timers keep tattered notebooks with lists of waypoints. This is probably a hangover from the days when Loran-C and Decca were in their infancy and data was stored in this way. People who have grown up with GPS rely on machine storage exclusively, but it can be tedious to scroll through a waypoint list number by number to get to the ones you want. A useful compromise is to have a loose-leaf waypoint directory with them grouped geographically or by their route numbers, and on page 57 is a suggested layout with number, name, location and latitude and longitude in the first five columns. The log reading, time, bearing and distance go in when the route is used. The last column is particularly useful when planning a voyage, for by totting up the distances and dividing the total by your boat's average speed, you can answer that constant question from crew and partners: 'how long will it be to the next port?'

**USING THE WAYPOINT DIRECTORY TO PLAN A VOYAGE**

A great deal of measuring distances from the chart may be avoided by putting the full directory entry to work. You have been this way once before and have completed the end columns giving bearing and distance which were blank originally. It is an October day with eleven and a half hours of daylight and your motor craft cruises comfortably at ten knots. Can you get from St Catherine's Point to Start Point in daylight with a smooth sea, little wind and good visibility?

From the last column of the waypoint directory you can see that the distances are 45.25 and 52.04 nm, making 97.29 nm altogether. Divide by 10 and the expected duration of a voyage from CAPO to STAR is just under ten hours. Yes, it can be done between dawn and dusk with a little in hand for an overnight berth at Salcombe.

**WAYPOINT AND ROUTE WORKING SHEET**

| No. | Name | Desc. | Lat. | Long. | Log | Time | Brg. | Dist. |
|---|---|---|---|---|---|---|---|---|
| 001 | NAB | SW of Nab Tower | 50° 37.00 N | 001° 02.00 W | | | | |
| 002 | CAPO | Off St. Catherine's Point | 50° 33.000 N | 001° 17.000 W | | | | |
| 003 | BILL | Off Portland Bill | 50° 25.000 N | 002° 27.000 W | | | | |
| 004 | STAR | Off Start Point | 50° 10.000 N | 003° 45.000 W | | | | |
| 005 | FALMO | Off Falmouth | 50° 06.050 N | 004° 56.000 W | | | | |
| 006 | LIZ | Off Lizard Point | 49° 56.000 N | 005° 12.000 W | | | | |
| 007 | WOLF | South of Wolf Rock | 49° 55.000 N | 005° 48.000 W | | | | |

**WAYPOINT AND ROUTE WORKING SHEET**

| No. | Name | Desc. | Lat. | Long. | Log | Time | Brg. | Dist. |
|---|---|---|---|---|---|---|---|---|
| 002 | CAPO | Off St. Catherine's Point | 50° 33.000 N | 001° 17.000 W | 2321 | 1906 | 265° | 45.25 |
| 003 | BILL | Off Portland Bill | 50° 25.000 N | 002° 27.000 W | 2366 | 2330 | 259° | 52.04 |
| 004 | STAR | Off Start Point | 50° 10.000 N | 003° 45.000 W | 2413 | 0410 | 271° | 46.58 |
| 005 | FALMO | Off Falmouth | 50° 06.050 N | 004° 56.000 W | | | | |

*MAKING A
ROUTE WITH
THE NAV 398*

Many English and Dutch yachtsmen make an annual trip to the Scilly Isles, going down-Channel to the westward in the Spring, when easterlies can be expected, and coming back later in the year. They choose legs that give a degree of straight-line sailing, but modified so that a port of refuge is not too far off the track. A multiple-leg route may be created. Start with  ROUTE 5   MAKE  3  ENTER , which brings up MAKE ROUTE ROUTE 3.

This is a return voyage, so when the machine shows a FROM, inviting waypoint numbers, a start is made with one off the Lizard. Put in  0  0  6  ENTER  followed by 0  0  5   ENTER  and the display brings up the first course and distance as:

BRG  050°  DTG  14.3 nm.

Touch the LEG soft key and insert  0  0  4  ENTER  for the next waypoint off Start Point. Another touch on the LEG soft key and  0  0  3  ENTER  completes the route from the Lizard to Portland Bill. A final  ENTER  takes you back to a POS display.

*USING THE
ROUTE*

You have the first course and distance, and turning on AUTO SEQUENCE brings up the next leg when the arrival alarm in Figure 13 goes off. To inspect any leg of the voyage touch  WPT 4   GOTO WPT LIST and scroll through with the  3  key. WPT 7 will be on the screen and a touch of  POS 1  brings up WPT 6 and the next one, WPT 5. Going the other way, the  CDI 3  key reveals the various legs of the route in turn.

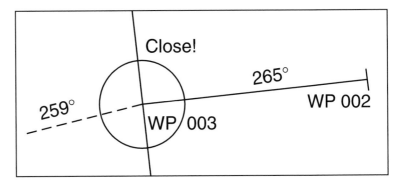

*Fig 13 The
arrival circle.*

*MAKING A ROUTE WITH THE 12XL*

Open-sea voyages can often be made with long straight legs between two waypoints, but an indented coast – such as that of western Ireland or Norway – requires the GPS set user to construct routes of two or more legs. Similarly, to get from NAB (waypoint 1) to BILL (waypoint 3) a turn must be made at CAPO (waypoint 2).

The entry procedure goes like this:  ON   WELCOME PAGE  × 7 discloses MENU and scroll ▼ or ▲ to ROUTES followed by  ENTER . The empty route definition page looks like this:

```
ROUTE                              (NO)


  -------------------------
  NO      WAYPNT        DTN    DST
  I
  2
  3
  4
  5
  6

  TOTAL DST                        0.00

                    COPY TO _ _ _ _
      CLR?          INV?           ACT?
```

Highlight the route number at top right, if not already highlighted, and  ENTER . Put in your number and  ENTER  again. Another  ENTER  is required to begin filling in the route comment line below using ▼ , ▲ and ▶ to make the line read something like NAB 2 BILL and  ENTER  it. Highlight 1 WAYPNT and  ENTER  it. Touch the ▼ and ▶ to insert the number and name for each waypoint with an

ENTER to start and finish each one. After the details of way-point 3 are in, key PAGE . When activated, the display shows:

| ROUTE | 5 | | |
|---|---|---|---|
| NAB | 2 | BILL | |
| NO | WAYPNT | DTN | DST |
| I | NAB | | |
| | | 252° | 10.33 |
| 2 | CAPO | | |
| | | 265° | 45.25 |
| 3 | BILL | | |
| 4 | | | |
| 5 | | | |
| 6 | | | |
| TOTAL DST | | | 55.58 |
| | COPY TO: | I? | |
| CLR? | | INV? | ACT? |

To activate the route select the route definition page and ENTER . Key in 5 for the number and ENTER . Use ▼ to highlight ACT? and ENTER . Key the left-facing arrow to CLR and use INV if you want to reverse the route and go from waypoint 3 to waypoint 1.

*A TRIANGULAR ROUTE*    Cruising people tend to go in straight lines, but the racing fra-ternity prefer triangular courses to test their craft on all points of sailing. This time it is a race from the entrance to Biscayne Bay to the waypoint off Gun Key to another off Port Everglades and back to Biscayne Bay, about 118 miles in all. The waypoint positions are:

| | | |
|---|---|---|
| Biscayne Bay entrance | N 25° 39.540′ | W 080° 02.710′ |
| Gun Key | N 25° 33.410′ | W 079° 18.890′ |
| Port Everglades | N 26° 05.898′ | W 080° 05.371′ |

and they have been put in the **Explorer**'s memory as waypoints 19, 20 and 21 respectively.

First, we number the route and give it a name, starting with PWR navigational warning EXIT MENU and highlighting PLAN/EDIT ROUTES. A ▶ and a route number appears, but it is taken. Go ▶ to find an EMPTY number and ENT it. ▼ to EDIT NAME and a ▶ gives the opportunity to key in BAH with ▲ and ▶ and ENT it. EXIT takes you back with a ▶ to the ROUTES page, which now has BAH at the top. Move to EDIT ROUTE and ▶ . The next page is for putting in the latitude and longitude of waypoint numbers with an ADD WPT each time until they are racked up in order with their bearings and distances.

It works out at just under 40 nm to Gun Key and just under 53 to Port Everglades, with the last leg about 26 nm. The first two courselines run 103° and 312°, but it is likely that the racing crew will eyeball the last leg back to Biscayne Bay entrance because of the proximity of the land to starboard. Additionally, with the Gulf Stream against them on the final leg it makes sense to look for back-eddies in the bights to beat the adverse current. This is one of the few instances where the GPS set does *not* give the best course to steer.

*CREATING A ROUTE WHILE ON PASSAGE*

Not all routes are set-piece affairs prepared in advance, for sailing craft may have to improvise if the wind is right in the teeth when they get clear of the land. Obviously, that means tacking either side of the courseline to get to the up-wind destination. Many, but not all, GPS sets have a bearing-and-distance facility that makes waypoints and a route from a single initial fix. The process is shown overleaf. Imagine that a yacht comes out of the marina and the owner/navigator finds to his total disgust that although he has only 36 miles to go, the wind is wholly adverse and is forecast to remain so.

The first step is to record your present position as a waypoint – a technique described at the beginning of Chapter 5. A sailing cruiser can make 45° to the wind with the sheets slightly eased. As the courseline is 225°, the tack headings will be 180° and 270° by turn. The first leg from waypoint 22 will be a southerly one of 5 nm and the GPS set is given a 180°

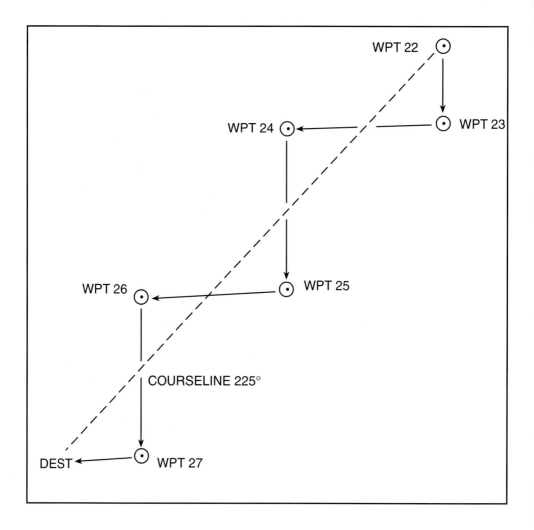

bearing and 5 so that it comes up with waypoint 23. When the arrival alarm goes off near that position it is time to go about and input a 270° bearing and ten miles of distance to create waypoint 24. Keep feeding the machine with ten miles and alternate westerly and southerly bearings until waypoint 27, when the final five miles to the west brings the yacht to its destination. If the prevailing wind is south-westerly and this is a regular trip, the route may be saved for next time.

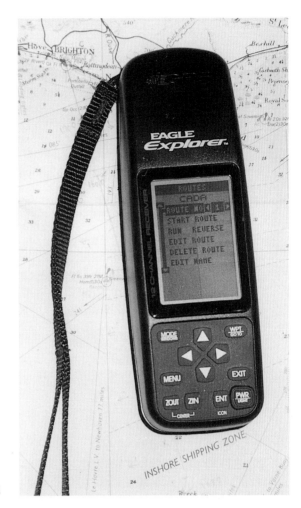

*Eagle Explorer.*

**HOW MANY ROUTES AND WAYPOINTS DO YOU NEED?**

By and large, the fixed sets have greater route and waypoint capacity than the hand-helds, but some of the latter run them close. The **Valsat SP** can cope with 20 routes of up to 20 waypoints each, and a clip-on pack gives another 1,000 waypoints. The **12XL** also has 20 routes which can hold 30 waypoints apiece, although few trips will require such a number. The **Sportsman** holds 500 waypoints in the memory and can make 9 routes. Surprisingly, the fixed **Fishfinder/Plotter 560** can hold only 200 waypoints, but that is probably because the manufacturer has slanted the product to appeal to fishfinders rather than position finders. So, how many of each do you need? Family sailors who get out for, perhaps, twelve weekends a year and one three-week annual cruise will be hard put to it to use more than 100 waypoints and 10 routes. From their perspective, the inexpensive set is as good as the latest state-of-the-art machine.

*DELETING A ROUTE*

To take a route out of the memory with the **Explorer**, key PWR navigational warning EXIT MENU and highlight PLAN/EDIT ROUTES. A ▶ presents a page with ROUTE 1 at the top and a number of choices, including DELETE ROUTE. A ▼ and a ▶ discloses the message ARE YOU SURE YOU WANT TO DELETE THIS ROUTE with YES and NO boxes right and left. A ▶ takes it out and a ◀ saves it from extinction.

The **12XL** has a similar cancellation message when a route has to go, starting with ON PAGE × 5 to MAIN MENU and ▼ to ROUTES and an ENTER . Put in the route number – 17 in this case – and ENTER . Scroll down to the bottom line and key ◀ CLR ENTER . The message reads WARNING – *all waypoints will be removed from this route*, so ◀ to YES and ENTER your decision.

Other sets will ask if you really want to delete a route and a positive YES is generally required.

# 7 • Cross Track Error and the Course to Steer

The waypoints and routes give the way we *ought* to go, and if voyages were always on a lake with no wind, nothing more would be needed. The bearing given by the GPS set is a planned direction of travel, but wind, wave and current will be combining to drive the boat off that courseline and making corrections will be quite a normal procedure. Let us see how various sets cope with them – and keep one eye on Figure 14, which explains the terms used.

*CROSS TRACK*
*ERROR*
*CORRECTIONS*
*WITH THE*
*ADMIRAL*

A NAV brings up a display showing range and bearing to the next waypoint and four soft key options. One of them is STEER, and a touch reveals the page below:

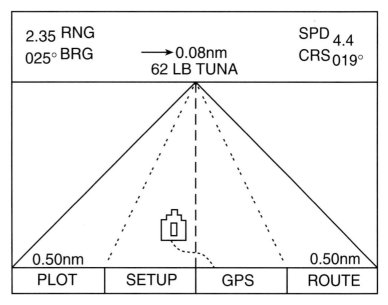

The centre dotted line is the courseline and the cursor looking like a miniature castle is the position of your craft in relation

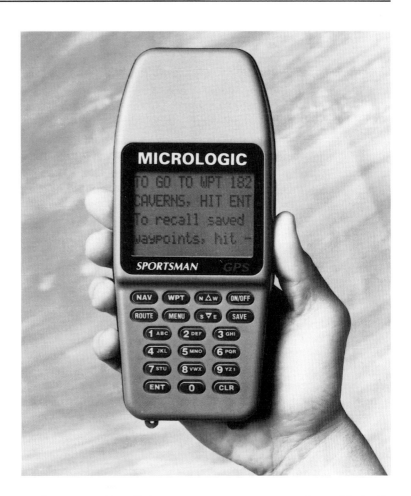

*The Micrologic
Sportsman.*

to that courseline. It is to port, so a turn to starboard is indicated. Range (distance) to the waypoint, its bearing, the speed
and present course are given at the top of the page. Top centre is an arrow showing that a turn to starboard is needed; the
accompanying figure shows that the craft is 0.08 nm off the
courseline – a mere 150 metres or so. The waypoint is about
2.3 nm away, according to the figure in the top left-hand corner of the page, and the important thing in this case is *not* to
overreact. A change of direction of, perhaps, three degrees to
starboard will suffice and the cross track error (XTE) reading
should reduce. If it doesn't, give it another couple of degrees.
The cursor will be of assistance when other matters claim

attention and the occasional check on XTE is required.

Having said that gentle corrections are always preferable to large ones, it is important to emphasize that there are exceptions. In Chapter 5 the courseline given by the **Sportsman** from the entrance to Biscayne Bay to Gun Key was 103°, but in this part of the world the Gulf Stream flows northwards like a river at all seasons and the navigator needs to make a decisive correction from the beginning, heading well out to starboard from the courseline to counteract the push of the current. A boat capable of 12 knots would have to steer 118° or 120° all the way *and* make frequent revision of the course at, say, half-hourly intervals. A yacht with less speed would have to steer even higher than 120° to stay with the courseline. When experience gives this kind of lesson, it makes sense to add an extra column to the Directory, or have a remarks page, so that you can use the best course to steer again next time.

***THE EXPLORER'S CDI AND XTK DISPLAY***

This set has a comprehensive eight-box display giving bearing, distance to go, track, ground speed, estimated time on route, course, course deviation indicator and cross track error, and it looks like this:

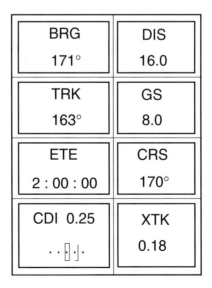

| BRG | DIS |
|-----|-----|
| 171° | 16.0 |
| TRK | GS |
| 163° | 8.0 |
| ETE | CRS |
| 2 : 00 : 00 | 170° |
| CDI  0.25 | XTK |
| . . ⟦·⟧· | 0.18 |

The page is arrived at with PWR navigational warning EXIT MODE ▲ ▶ EXIT . The CDI at bottom left has a vertical line. If it is central, you are on the courseline. If not, there is cross track error and the XTK box at bottom right tells you by how much. The default setting is a quarter of a mile, and to change the CDI range, touch PWR navigational warning EXIT MENU and ▲ to ALARMS/CDI. A ▶ brings a page with CDI DIST 0.25 nm at its foot, and ▼ get there with ◀ or ▶ to change the figure to the required range in 0.05 nm intervals.

*THE COURSE DEVIATION INDICATOR OF THE FISHFINDER/ PLOTTER 560*

This neat layout is arrived at with PWR NAVIGATION MENU ▶ NAVIGATION ▶ NAV 2, and it appears in the drawing below. The dotted courseline is central with the aimed-for waypoint at the top. Arrows and STEER show the way the boat must go to get back to the courseline. The layout gives, from bottom left round to bottom right, the GPS position and the grade of fix followed by the depth. The course-made-good, velocity to destination, or speed, come next and the route number. Under the XTE grid there is the amount of error and, in the corner, the bearing and range. If a constant falling-off to port is experienced, there is another way to correct the heading. The 7 EVENT button gives

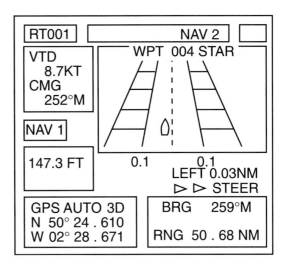

present position as a waypoint. If it is followed by 6 GOTO and keying in the destination waypoint number – 004 – and ▶ ENTER , a new bearing and range will show up. In strong tides flowing at different rates and directions, this is the best procedure, and, when used in conjunction with an off-course alarm, will give good results. The CDI scale is set to 0.1 nm but other settings are often possible. The **12XL**, for example, has 0.25 nm, 1.25 and 5 nm on call. To change from 0.25 nm, the default setting, key ON WELCOME PAGE PAGE PAGE PAGE PAGE PAGE PAGE ▼ NAV ENTER to get to NAV SETUP. ▼ ▼ ▼ highlights SCALE and the default 0.25 figure. To change it, key ENTER ▼ ▼ to get 1.25 nm and ▼ ▼ again to arrive at 5nm and ENTER accordingly.

*TERMS*
*EXPLAINED*

This is a good time to get some of the terms used in the manuals sorted into categories, for manufacturers tend to employ words supplied by the boffins with minimum explanation. Look at Figure 16 and run through it from the bottom.

**BRG**[1] is the magnetic bearing supplied by the unit to get from WP 02 to WP 03.

**XTE** represents the effect of wind blowing from the west and pushing the boat off the courseline to the east.

**Distance Made Good (DMG)** is represented, after the amount of XTE is established, by the line joining WP 02 and the ship.

**Course Made Good (CMG)** is the angle in degrees between the north pointer and the DMG line. Above the XTE line in Figure 14 there is a double dotted line break to show that **Velocity Made Good (VMG)** is the speed as it would be measured along this piece of courseline from the XTE join to the dotted line.

**Speed Over the Ground (SOG)** is measured from the ship towards WP 03 and is the *actual* ground speed when the dotted line is reached.

**BRG**[2] is the new courseline for WP 03.

**Course Over the Ground (COG)** is put in to show what happens if you don't make enough allowance for XTE.

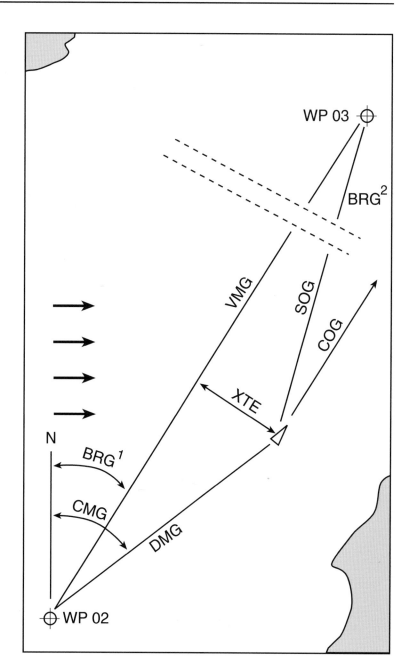

***Fig 14*** *Some terms used in GPS navigation.*

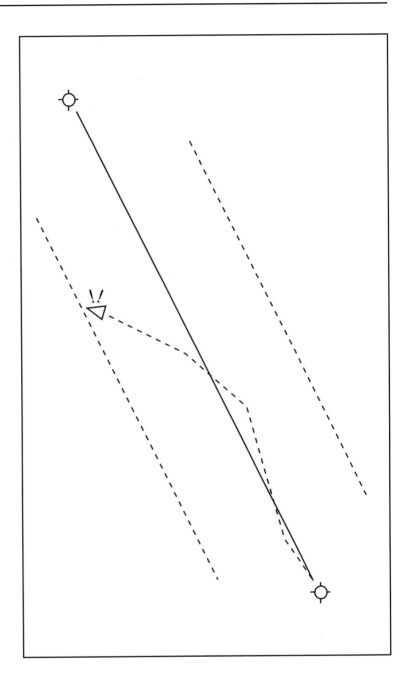

**Fig 15** *Crossing the XTE alarm line.*

The GPS user has changed course to port, but the wind is still pushing the boat sideways so that the 'new' COG is parallel to the old courseline and another alteration will be needed to close WP 03. Many of the terms that have been coined in recent years use speed and velocity as interchangeable, so that Velocity Over the Ground (VOG) is the same as ground speed, while with some sets, you actually get SOG if you touch   VEL  . It is always best to assimilate as many of the manufacturer's meanings for functions as you can before getting down to serious work with an actual set.

*THE OFF-*
*COURSE*
*ALARM AND*
*ALARM LINES*

So far, we have assumed that the attentive navigator is keeping an eye on the heading and making corrections when his craft strays too far from the courseline, but a useful back-up at night or in rough weather is the off-course alarm that beeps or flashes when the boat strays too far from that line. Figure 15 demonstrates the principle. All sets have a SET ALARMS mode inviting you to enter a distance from the courseline to serve as an alarm boundary. The **Explorer** starts with  PWR  navigational warning  EXIT   MENU  and then you have  ▲  to select ALARMS/CDI. A  ▶  and  ▼  take you to CDI ALARM, which should be keyed from OFF to ON if necessary. Go  ▼  to CDI DIST and highlight it. Use  ◀  or  ▶  to vary the alarm distance from the default figure in units of 0.05 nm.

# 8 • Loran-C Backup and Fishfinder Use

In Chapter 1 the point was made that while a Global Navigation Satellite System (GNSS) lies in the near future, the present reality is that America's GPS and Russia's GLONASS can be switched off at will. The obvious corollary is that yachtsmen need an alternative electronic fixing system. A year or two ago there was a struggle between Omega, Decca and Loran-C for primacy as the principal back-up to GPS. The result was that Loran-C, a hyperbolic radio network of land-based stations, was the victor.

Loran-C operates through regionalised chains of stations, with each chain comprising one master and several slave, or secondary, stations transmitting pulse groups at what are called Group Repetition Intervals so that chains are identified by their GRIs in microseconds reduced to a four-figure number. A list of the chains and their GRIs appears in Appendix 2.These signals are logged at the receiver by Time Differences (TDs).

As signal speed over the surface of the earth is constant, or nearly so, and the stations are at accurately-plotted locations, the TDs can be turned into distance and provide a fix. The range of signals is between 800 and 1200 nm, so Loran-C is not effective everywhere, and there is inevitable distortion when signals pass over land. On the other hand, the system is relatively inexpensive and remains very popular with light aircraft pilots and fishermen.

At the time of writing, Loran-C has partly cast off the sheltering embrace of the United States Coast Guard and two regional groups have taken over control in their areas. The North-west European Loran Service (NELS) and the Far-Eastern Radionavigation Service (FERNS) operate as a species of international co-operative with no user costs. The proposed European Radionavigation Plan (ERNP) envisages a fully integrated navaid system combining GPS, GLONASS, LORAN-C and CHAYKA – the Russian equivalent – but, as things stand, the problem of legal liability and the high standards required by commercial aviation has yet to be overcome. In the meantime, manufacturers have developed combined GPS/LORAN-C receivers, and the **NAV 398** is an example of the hybrid receiver using a separate sensor for Loran-C signals.

The set starts in the usual way with   PWR LITE  . After the testing process, the screen fills with an entry headed SIGNAL STATUS LORAN. It is important to study the display because it will tell you whether or not there is going to be a satisfactory match for a fix. First, in the usual way, it is necessary to tell the unit roughly where it is and touch EST  ▶, the top soft key, to put in the approximate latitude and longitude with   ENTER  s until the status page appears again. It will look something like this:

| SIGNAL STATUS LORAN | | | |
|---|---|---|---|
| GRI = 7499A | SNR | TRK | EST▶ |
| M      OSC = -18 | 51 | 8 | |
| S1     12302.5 | 88 | 8 | |
| S2     30890.6 | 30 | 8 | |
| S3     00000.0 | 00 | 00 | STA▶ |
| S4     00000.0 | 00 | 00 | |
| S5     00000.0 | 00 | 00 | |
| EST      N 51 15.33′ | | | ECD▶ |
| POS    W 001 37.37′ | | | |
| PRESS CLEAR TO EXIT | | | |

Top left is the GRI, which is also the chain number, and an A to show that this is the machine's automatic selection of the best signal response. Had you selected one manually by presses of STA ▶ , the letter M would show here. The figures following S1 and S2 are the TDs for the secondaries and the

*Raytheon Marine Company NAV 398 GPS/Loran.*

SNR numbers give the signal-to-noise ratio. This describes signal strength in relation to background noise. Anything over 70 is good, over 50 is fair and under 50 is poor. The TRK readings of 8 show that three stations have locked-on and a fix is on the cards. A further status check is made by touching the ECD ▶ soft key so that:

|    |    |
|----|----|
| M  | 70 |
| S1 | 90 |
| S2 | 40 |

appears in the former SNR column. ECD stands for Envelope-to-Cycle Difference and is a measure of signal matching, with 50 being very good, 20 to 80 fair and 0 to 10 and 90 to 99 unreliable. S1 has a feeble ECD figure but a good SNR, and S2 a poor SNR but a good ECD, so it seems worthwhile to go for a fix with CLR CLR . The display brings up:

N   51° 15.28′
W  001° 37.84′

which differs only a little from the back-garden GPS fix

obtained in Chapter 5. The reasons for the discrepancy are probably that the station at Sylt is some way off, all the signals have passed over land and S1, in particular, was marginal for a good result. Nevertheless, it is a reasonable back-up fix for a GPS owner temporarily deprived of signals. Can the **NAV 398** and Loran-C sensor cope with waypoints stored for GPS use? Yes, if the simulator is used. Start with PLOT 8 mode and touch MENU , the SIMULATOR soft key and CLR . Next, tap in GOTO 7 0 0 4 ENTER and the top of the display shows BRG 168° DTG 44.6 nm (this is the same bearing as provided by the GPS for the one-leg voyage between HOME and CAPO but the distance-to-go is 0.4 nm further). To get the very best results from the Loran-C sensor it is necessary to follow the complete initialization sequence when the GPS sensor is connected. After the latitude and longitude have gone in, plus antenna height, date and time, follow the prompt for the Loran-C data. This consists of the GRI number and the first two digits of the secondary station TDs. For example, having entered 7499 for the GRI, put in 1 2 ENTER for S1 and 3 0 ENTER for S2 and reasonable accuracy can be guaranteed.

**RELIABILITY OF LORAN-C**

Is Loran-C foolproof? The system gives repeatable accuracy, which is what fishermen prize most highly, but accidents do happen. Some years ago the transmitting tower at Kargabarun in Turkey fell down and cover in the eastern Mediterranean ceased abruptly. Sailors found that once they were east of Crete there was no reliable fix between there and the coast of Israel. The problem was to last for many months as argument raged as to who was to pay for repairs. Now that control is passing from the United States Coast Guard to nations and nation groups, it is salutary to bear in mind that even the back-up fails occasionally. Another problem arises when your position is in line with, but beyond, the baseline joining a master station and a secondary. What happens is that the TDs are so widely spaced along the baseline extension that Loran-C fixes are unreliable – as in Figure 16. This phenomena is particularly annoying between the toe and heel of Italy, so when sailing

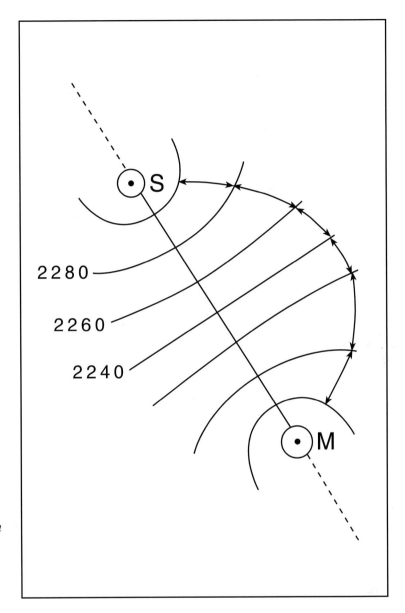

**Fig. 16** *The gradients between TDs get larger as the dotted baseline extension gets closer.*

eastwards from Crotone it is best to ignore Loran-C fixes until well up to the island of Corfu. Similar difficulties may be experienced off Nantucket and south of Charleston and east of Savannah.

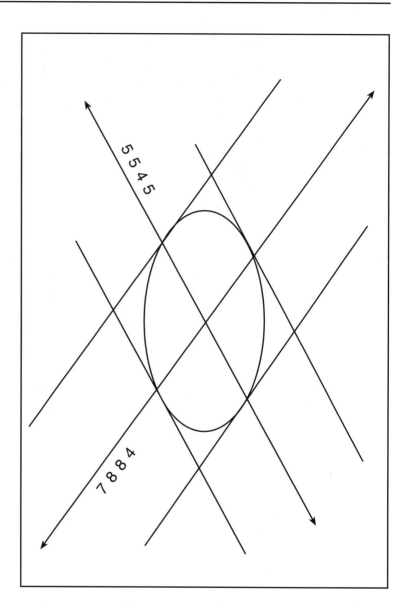

**Fig 17** *The probability ellipse for two Loran-C position lines at long range.*

**ACCURACY OF A LORAN-C FIX**

A fix from two position lines becomes less accurate as the distance from the transmitters increases. A 95 per cent probability ellipse, as shown in Figure 17, represents the amount of likely error at long range. The ellipse is roughly the

*Apelco 560
Fishfinder/Plotter
with Forward
Looking display.*

same area as the diamond formed by the probability bands on each side of the position lines, and at a narrow angle of cut, the error will be larger. As a general rule, allow 200 metres of error for a fix from Loran-C – just as you would for a GPS fix.

***UNDERWATER
MODE OF THE
FISHFINDER /
PLOTTER 560***

The GPS functions of this set have already been covered and it only remains to describe its underwater and plotting capacity. Connected to a through-hull or through-transom transducer, the unit responds to presses on the top soft key and the fishfinder menu to bring up a display showing the depth in feet and a contoured seabed. Further keying gives the water temperature, the GPS position in latitude and longitude, speed and the distance logged. A waypoint window shows the bearing and range to the next waypoint. A forward-looking mode is available and, best of all, an indication of the nature of the bottom through a high-resolution display (see Figure 18). Hard sand appears as a thin line, soft mud is thicker and rocks or wrecks are irregular and jagged in form.

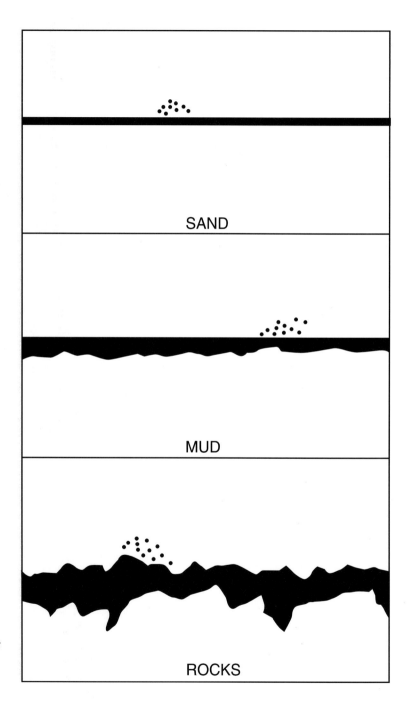

*Fig 18* *The three main types of bottom contour.*

SAND

MUD

ROCKS

This is useful knowledge when anchoring the boat in a place where you have not anchored before.

Fishermen like to know what their chances are at a new location and the set shows individual fish in the sounding beam. It was thoughtful of the designers to embody fish symbols in six sizes so that the little ones can be ignored and a fish alarm detects anything not attached to the bottom so that the operator does not have to stare at the display for long periods. In plot mode a wreck or shoal can be named as a waypoint so that a circling craft finds its way back to the action. The basic operation starts at the main menu display and the middle soft key gives plot mode. The split screen permits the plot and forward beam to co-exist, although it must be borne in mind that the forward beam is narrow and will not show rocks located in front of you and just below the surface. When done with, a touch of  MODE  will return the display to main menu.

## 9 • *Desirable Optional Extras*

All GPS sets provide position on demand and a bearing and distance between waypoints, but many embody special features as a selling point and to be one up on rivals. We benefit from competition of this kind and this chapter deals with the various extras that manufacturers have provided.

*LIGHTS AND BUOYS IN THE MEMORY*

Micrologic's **Admiral** has a built-in database with the name, location and characteristics of lights and buoys in a given area. This is in addition to the waypoints put in the memory by the navigator and when ordering a unit you can specify which area will be the venue for the set. The European version has over 13,000 lights and buoys in the memory; the Pacific database less than half that number. This feature comes into its own on dark nights and approaching land, when several touches of  WPT  brings up a display giving the nearest light:

| LIGHT  L | | 1st closest  4320         to PP  LITTLE RIVER | |
|---|---|---|---|
| N | 44° 39.000′ | | |
| W | 067° 11.500′ | | |
| R    13 nm | | CHAR FL W 6s | |
| RNG      1.22 nm | | BRG      352°      mag | |
| | DBASE | | MOVE |

Using the plus key, up to 20 lights can be found with their bearing, distance and latitude and longitude from the number above the name. Buoys are summoned with  WPT   WPT   WPT  and a lighted buoy can be added if, for example, it is a new mark not already in the memory.

*ADDING A LIGHTED BUOY TO THE DATABASE*

Let us imagine that a navigator wants to add a useful channel buoy that he uses regularly. It is at latitude N 42° 46.312′ and longitude W 070° 29.671′, has a green light that flashes every two seconds and can be seen for about a mile. (Note here that the entries are alphanumeric – mixed letters and figures requiring repeated presses of the keys.) To get to the database page touch  WPT  WPT  WPT  and DBASE on the soft key, followed by  CLR  1ABC  ENT  to give a number, and then enter the name:

| CLR | 1ABC | 1ABC | 1ABC | N+W | 3GHI | 3GHI |
|-----|------|------|------|------|------|------|
| N+W | 1ABC | N+W | 8VWX | 8VWX | N+W | ENT |

followed by the latitude and longitude:

| CLR | 4JKL | 2DEF | 4JKL | 6PQR | 3GHI | 1ABC |
|-----|------|------|------|------|------|------|
| 2DEF | ENT | CLR | 0 | 7STU | 0 | 2DEF |
| 9YZ | 6PQR | 7STU | 1ABC | ENT | | |

and add the visibility range with  CLR  1ABC  ENT  and the light characteristics as:

| CLR | 2DEF | 2DEF | 2DEF | N+W | 4JKL | 4JKL | 4JKL |
|-----|------|------|------|------|------|------|------|
| N+W | N+W | 3GHI | N+W | N+W | 2DEF | 2DEF | 2DEF |
| 2DEF | 2DEF | 2DEF | N+W | 7STU | ENT | | |

so that the buoy coded CHAW is in the memory and will be shown on the page with a B symbol when required.

*MAN OVER-BOARD*

This alarm is often given a great deal of emphasis in the sales literature and with the **Admiral** and the **Sportsman** a touch on  SAVE  SAVE  does two things: the position is recorded and the display shows the course back to it. The chief value of the man overboard feature in most GPS sets is that the position is treated as a waypoint. If rescue craft have to be called in following a MAYDAY on the VHF set, they have a fix serving as the centre of a rescue pattern. Other sets, like the **NAV**

**398**, have a dedicated  MOB  button that has the same function. It is often given a different colour to make it stand out from the others. The **NAV 398** gives the man overboard position as waypoint 999 and the plot shows a dotted line joining your craft to the splashpoint with BRG and DTG back to it. The scale is 0.5 nm, to allow for any delay between man overboard and the  MOB  button being pressed, and the arrival alarm goes off at 0.1 nm from that position. The **Valsat SP** operates on three levels. In level 1 a  MARK  discloses a centre of uncertainty, with MOB at its centre and a bearing and distance back to that centre. For levels 2 and 3 it has to be  MARK   MARK   MARK . If in doubt, always press three times as the display will not change even if level 1 is being employed.

*CHANGES IN DEPTH UNITS, DISTANCE, TEMPERA-TURE AND LANGUAGE*

The **Fishfinder/Plotter 560** has an easy procedure for these changes using SET UP and it is possible to change depth units from feet to metres, temperature from Fahrenheit to Celsius and languages from English to German, French, Spanish, Norwegian or Italian. Start with  PWR   9 SET UP   ▼   NEXT to disclose DEPTH UNIT and TEMP UNIT and use the  ► soft key to change feet to metres and Fahrenheit to Celsius. A touch on  ▼  NEXT  ▼  NEXT calls up LANGUAGE and  ► ►  changes ENGLISH to FRENCH. Keying  ►   ►   ►   ► returns the language to ENGLISH once more. It is not wise to assume that a new set has nautical miles as the default setting because at least one – the **12XL** – comes from the factory with statute miles as distance measurement. The change to nautical miles is accomplished by  ON   WELCOME   PAGE  × 7 and  ▼  NAVIGATION  ENTER . Scroll  ▼  to UNITS and choose either  M ETRIC or  N AUTICAL and  ENTER  the new distance criteria for use.

*SIMULATORS*

A set with a simulator enables the yachtsman to practise keying at home and the **12XL** starts achieving that mode in the same way as with distance units by beginning with  ON  WELCOME  PAGE  × 7 to MENU. Scroll  ▼  to SYSTEM so that an  ENTER  reveals SYSTEM SETUP. Scroll  ▲  or  ▼  to get to

MODE Normal and ENTER once more. The 'N' in Normal is highlighted and a ▼ changes the reading to S imulator? ENTER it and return to the MENU display with PAGE. When the machine goes off the set returns to normal operation at once, so if you intend to have a lengthy session at home, leave the set on all the time. The simulator built into the **Explorer** is triggered by PWR navigation warning EXIT MENU and ▼ to SIMULATOR SETUP. A ▶ changes OFF to ON. A peculiarity with this set is that the default speed setting is 100 miles an hour and highlighting SPEED permits a lower figure with ◀ and ▶. When you have got it right, touch ENTER.

*ANCHOR*
*ALARM*

This useful device gives warning if a boat drifts more than a specified distance from the anchoring position. Figure 19 shows alarm circles set at 0.03 and 0.06 nm, which is about 56 and 111 metres respectively. However, these may be a little tight when wind and tide are strong and some sets, like the **Sportsman**, have a minimum radius of 0.1 nm. To set the anchor alarm, start with: MENU MENU MENU MENU which brings up TO SEE SETUP DISPLAYS PRESS + and a N+W shows:

| alerts | on/off | nm |
|--------|--------|-------|
| ARRIVAL | OFF | 0.05 |
| ANCHOR | OFF | 0.10 |
| CTE | OFF | +0.10 |

CLR s turn ANCHOR OFF to ANCHOR ON and the default radius of 0.1 nm can go in with an ENT. If the anchored craft drags beyond that distance from the anchoring position, an alarm sounds and the screen will read

ANCHOR WATCH ALERT, PRESS CLR.

The alarm sounds for four seconds and switch-off is accomplished with a CLR. A tenth of a mile is only a little under 200 metres and it will almost certainly be necessary to re-lay the anchor.

*AVOID AND PROXIMITY ALARMS*

These are very similar in operation to arrival or waypoint alarms which tell you that you are close to the destination waypoint, except that it is hazards that are marked. The **12XL** can hold nine proximity alarms in the memory and if you cross the alarm circle a message comes up reading something like PROX alarm – WOLF. To set the proximity alarm touch ON to get WELCOME and key PAGE PAGE PAGE PAGE PAGE PAGE PAGE to reveal the MENU. Scroll up or down to PROXIMITY WPTS and ENTER it. Highlight the first empty line and ENTER . Use ▲ or ▼ to go through the stored waypoints and ENTER the right one. The distance (DST) field is highlighted, so put in the desired alarm figure, say 0.25 nm, and close with a final ENTER . The **Admiral** has an audible avoid alarm and it is set by NAV SETUP AVOID followed by a latitude and longitude and an opportunity to choose a range. This could be 0 3 0 ENT to give 0.3 nm warning of the danger.

*THE BOUNDARY AND SHALLOW WATER ALARMS*

A refinement on the proximity alarm, the boundary alarm works by putting waypoints each side of a danger, joining them with a courseline and putting alarms of the XTE type parallel to that courseline. Figure 20 gives the principle and shows the practical application to the Wolf Rocks, which lie south-west to north-east in the path of shipping. A waypoint to the south-west at N 51° 05.10´, W 12° 43.22´ and another to the north-east at N 51° 08.95´, W 12° 39.90´ span the limits of the reef. The waypoints have generous alarm circles so as to create wide boundary alarms. Another desirable extra in some GPS sets is the shallow alarm that can be pre-set and buzzes when the contour line is reached. This alarm comes into its own when craft are closing a shelving shore to anchor. It is also popular with fishermen who want to find the fringe of a shoal where fish will be feeding.

*INTEGRAL AND ADD-ON PLOTTERS*

The plots that appear on the pages of your set give a birds-eye view of track and present position in one form and track, present position, a waypoint you are heading for and the projected courseline to get to it in a more elaborate version.

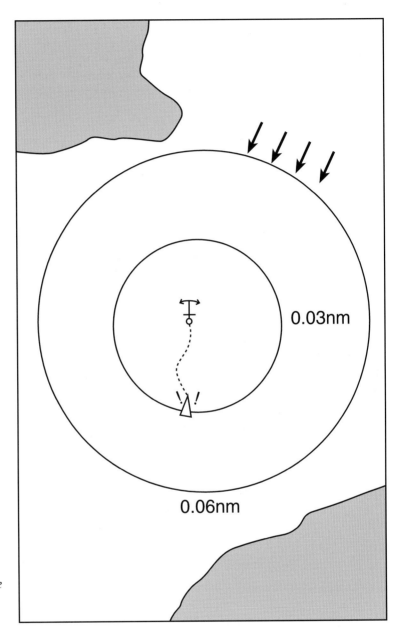

**Fig 19** *Tight alarm circles make for disturbed nights.*

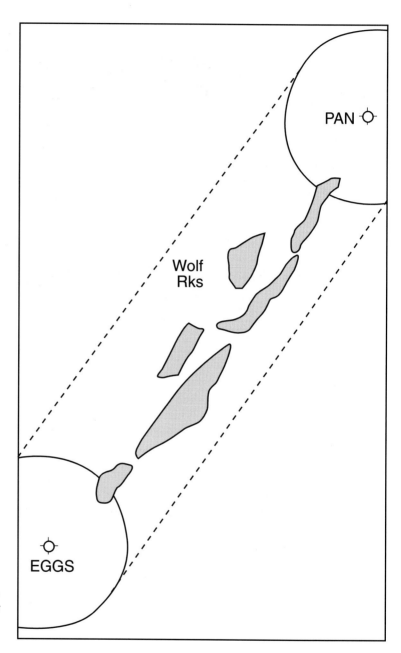

*Fig 20 Boundary alarms warning of rocks.*

*The 10 inch Navcenter Chartplotter from Autohelm.*

Most plots are north-up, as in an atlas, but a few have an up-track or an up-course mode. A cursor may be used to put in waypoints and the scale is adjustable from 0.1 nm upwards. They are informative but require a deal of peering to reveal that information. Their chief use is as a historical trail to show where you have just been and fishermen use them to get back to a spot where there was a nibble a short while back. For serious work you need an add-on electronic plotter with a screen at least seven inches across. Top of the range is the ten-inch plotter from Autohelm shown in the photograph above. It uses C-Map microcartridges, is fully waterproof and accepts position inputs from GPS and Loran-C.

# 10 • Faults, Accuracy and Other Uses of GPS

Sending the set back to the firm that sold it, or to the manufacturer, can be an expensive business so before taking that step do your own checks. The table opposite has general instructions for fault-finding and specifics for one set follow.

*TROUBLE-SHOOTING WITH THE FISHFINDER/ PLOTTER 560*

Trouble comes under three main headings: no signal, loss of memory and no power. When no signal is being received the first step is to check that the estimated latitude and longitude is right for your sea area and that time, date and year have been properly entered, then do a Hard Re-set. With the unit switched off press `PWR` and `3` simultaneously. This will erase all waypoints and routes and when the main menu appears follow the initialization routine described in Chapter 3.

If the memory goes, do a Hard Re-set and check the power supply for surges. If transient spikes show up, indicating power surges, instal filtering on the input DC power connections. When there is no power at all check the polarity of the DC cables and reverse them if necessary. Check the in-line fuse, replacing it if defective, and test the boat battery to make sure it is delivering voltage readings of 11 – 16V DC.

*ACCURACY*

In Chapter 1 there was a preliminary examination of sources of error and standards of accuracy, and in resuming the theme we must start with the awkward truth that charts printed before GPS existed were based on many datum positions and some were compiled with primitive instruments by men with little fundamental knowledge of the surveying art. For example, it has only recently been established that Pago Pago airport in the South Pacific is a good mile out of position, while some of the Caroline Islands are said to be as much as

| POSSIBLE FAULTS AND REMEDIES | |
| --- | --- |
| **Problem** | **Possible solution** |
| No power | Check switches and fuses. Are the wires leading to the battery loose? Some sets have a 2 amp fuse in the battery lead: check that it hasn't blown. |
| Dim display | Are the batteries failing? Check the contrast and dim key in case it's *your* fault. |
| Not receiving | Check satellite status; is the geometry right? Is antenna connected and does it need repositioning? |
| Latitude and longitude do not change | Ensure that initialization process has taken. If you are more than two degrees of latitude or longitude from where you switched off, do the start-up routine again. |
| Constant error in latitude and longitude | Is the HDOP figure wrong at this time of day? |
| Waypoints, bearings and distances are wrong | Are you on Auto MAG instead of TRUE? Has your boat crossed a meridian so that east/west error may be responsible? |
| Flashing display | Unreliable for navigation. Switch off and try again later. Check initialization if flashing continues. |
| Interference | Move antenna; change power source if you can. Switch off other power-users – eg fridges and strip lighting. Check that ground wire is connected. Move set temporarily away from compass. |

three miles from their true position according to the old charts. It follows that GPS-obtained positions are most accurate when plotted on charts based on modern surveys and the top grade standard is termed World Geodetic System 1984, or WGS 84 for short. Your charts may be newly printed but, sometimes, the datum on which they are based is older. A British Admiralty chart may bear the legend 'Positions obtained from satellite navigation systems are normally referred to WGS 72 datum; such positions should be moved 0.05 minutes NORTHWARD and 0.09 minutes EASTWARD to agree with this chart'. An American chart purchased in 1992 had a notice reading:

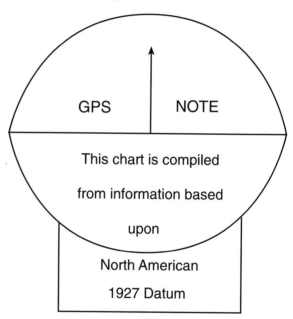

which is well before GPS-based position-finding was even thought of. The answer to this problem is to let the GPS adjust the readings so that what comes out needs no correction. If you do not allow the set to know the right chart datum, the worst scenario is that fixes could be 600 metres out.

*SELECTING THE RIGHT DATUM*

Most sets have a menu of ten or twelve datum references to match those on charts and maps. The common ones are:

| | |
|---|---|
| WGS 84 | (Often on sets when purchased ) |
| WGS 72 | (An older standard associated with earlier electronic systems such as Loran-C) |
| AUST 66 | (Australia) |
| NAD 27 | (Older American charts) |
| NAD 83 | (The American equivalent of WGS 84) |
| NAD 27 CAN | (Canada and Alaska) |
| EUROPEAN 50 | (Europe) |
| GD 49 | (New Zealand) |
| OSGB 36 | (Ordnance Survey, Great Britain) |
| BESSEL | (Japan) |

Two examples follow showing datum changes from WGS 84.

*CHANGE OF DATUM WITH THE SPORTS-MAN*

Let us imagine being in Australia and seeking to match a chart or map compiled according to AUST 66 datum. Switch on and key  MENU   MENU   N+W  × 7 to disclose:

```
MGRS/UTM         OFF
LORAN TD         OFF
MAP DATUM
MANU             WGS 84
```

A  CLR  × 4 brings up AUSTRALIA and further presses on the + key give AUSTR 66, which may be confirmed with an  ENT . To get back to WGS 84 use the  −  sign and end with another ENT when you reach it. In the second example we will go for the same datum using another set.

*DATUM CHANGE WITH THE NAV 398*

Start with  MENU  and then touch the NAV SETUPS soft key followed by POSITION CORR to get:

```
POSITION CORR
     GEODETIC SYSTEM      ▶
             WGS 84
```

at the top of the screen. Scrolling through with the soft key-opposite GEODETIC SYSTEM will reveal AUSTRA 66. To go back to WGS 84 continue with the soft key until it appears.

*GOING THE
OTHER WAY*

A change the other way may be needed with sets like the **Valsat SP**, which comes with EUROPEAN 50 as the default setting. To move to WGS 84 key PAGE × 8 and get to a display with MENU LEVEL at the top and MENU PAGE 27 in the bar at the bottom. Scroll down with ▼ × 4 and highlight MENU PAGE 27. ENTER ENTER brings up 16 datum choices, including WGS 84, and use the ▲ to get to it. A last ENTER confirms the change.

The **Explorer** may arrive from the dealer with a land coordinate setting or one based on the Military Grid Reference System (MRGS) and there has to be an alteration to degrees and minutes for use at sea. To make it, start with PWR navigation warning EXIT MENU ▲ SYSTEM SETUP ► GPS SETUP ►. A ▼ and ► are used to highlight POSITION FORMAT and there is a choice with ▲s to move to DM (degrees and minutes). The MGRS page is arrived at by the same process as far as the page used to achieve DM followed by ▲s to get to the MGRS alternatives. If, for example, the set is being used on a boat in Northern Ireland and the Irish Military Grid Reference System shows on the page, go ▼ to DM and confirm with ENT ENT EXIT .

*OTHER
GEODETIC
SYSTEMS*

There are, of course, many other datum references and a list appears in Appendix 1. For the British user of a GPS set the important one is OSGB 36, which may be employed with land maps when hill-walking or mountaineering. Hikers on a circular ramble on, say, Dartmoor can register their starting position in the car park as a waypoint and, when fog shrouds out the landscape, get a bearing and distance back to the starting point at the touch of a button. Lake fishermen use GPS sets to get back to that spot in the reeds where the big 'uns are lurking and backpack DGPS sets are being used for determining the extent of weeds in farmers' fields so that it is only necessary to apply herbicide to the weedy patches. It seems likely that governments paying subsidies to farmers are going to issue officials with GPS sets so that a check can be made on how many hectares or acres actually contain the subsidised crop. Looking further ahead, it seems entirely possible that post codes will give way to numbers for every address in the world – provided that the Selective Availability barrier can be overcome.

*ROAD VEHICLE AND PEDESTRIAN NAVIGATION*

GPS has been pressed into service as an aid to routeing road vehicles by means of turn-by-turn instruments allied to special street or motorway maps. The maps previously in use did not indicate one-way streets or pedestrianised roads, lanes and alleys too narrow for cars and trucks, and the data had to be gathered by teams and then digitised. Embodied in a CD-ROM, it was then tested for accuracy so that when the machine says 'turn right in fifty metres' it is feasible to do so. At the time of writing, turn-by-turn navigation has a database that includes all motorways and 'A' and 'B' roads in mainland Britain, together with over 300 urban centres – including London, the West Midlands, Manchester and Tyne and Wear. Of course, the database has to be updated continuously and there are plans to expand the use of this GPS system by recording and storing what is called 'point of interest' information, such as the whereabouts of post offices, railway stations and garages. When that happens the mass appeal will be greatly enhanced. GPS is being used in bus operations to convey information as to expected time of arrival and overhead signs tell passengers how long they have to wait. Speech messages giving the same information are being developed. Road patrols already use GPS with a CD-ROM database to find their way to broken-down motorists and the next step is to have cars fitted with a satellite-linked navigator so that a call by mobile telephone comes up as a precise location at the road patrol base and the patrol vehicle on the ground saves time in reaching it. The MoBIC system (Mobility of Blind and elderly people Interacting with Computers) gives precise directions from, say, home to the shops for pedestrians. A combination of a computer in a rucksack, headset, receiver and keypad strapped to the wrist accepts satellite signals to track the pedestrian's whereabouts as the computer gives precise spoken directions. MoBIC has had six months of testing in Birmingham and is going to be introduced for wider use in Europe.

**TRACKING ANIMALS AND HUMANS**

Rare animals fitted with collar sets are already being tracked and their habitat defined in national parks, and the Department of Comparative Animal Science at the University of Pisa is making an interesting study of the movements of a species of turtle. A female called Adelita (see photograph) has been fitted with a Platform Transmitting Terminal (PTT) using the Argos system of satellite telemetry to test the theory that these animals migrate half-way round the world to reproduce.

Stolen cars broadcast their whereabouts, and that of the thief, while a combined GPS set and cellular telephone will enable head office to know if a salesman is on the job or in the pub. So far, the civil liberties lobby has paid little attention to GPS but that is likely to change when, as seems inevitable, criminals and parolees will routinely be required to wear

*Adelita and her transmitter.*

bracelets giving police knowledge of their whereabouts at all times. In the same way that lorry drivers objected to the tachometer, calling it 'the spy in the cab', so there will be murmurings about GPS – 'the spy in the sky'.

**FUTURE DEVELOPMENTS**    The long-promised public and free DGPS service for United Kingdom waters begins with experimental transmissions from the six starred stations in the list below in May 1998. It is anticipated that all twelve stations will be working by the end of 1998, and WGS 84 datum matches and gives an estimated ten-metre accuracy for 95% of the time.

| Name | Location | | Frequency (KHz) |
|---|---|---|---|
| * North Foreland | 51° 23´ N | 01° 27´ E | 310.5 |
| * St Catherine's Point | 50° 35´ N | 01° 18´ W | 293.5 |
| * Lizard | 49° 58´ N | 05° 12´ W | 284.0 |
| * Nash Point | 51° 24´ N | 03° 33´ W | 299.0 |
| * Point Lynas | 53° 25´ N | 04° 17´ W | 305.0 |
| * Flamborough Head | 54° 07´ N | 00° 05´ W | 302.5 |
| Girdle Ness | 57° 08´ N | 02° 03´ W | 311.0 |
| Sumburgh Head | 59° 51´ N | 01° 16´ W | 304.0 |
| Butt of Lewis | 58° 31´ N | 06° 16´ W | 294.0 |
| Mizen Head | 51° 27´ N | 09° 49´ W | 300.5 |
| Loop Head | 52° 34´ N | 09° 56´ W | 312.0 |
| Tory Island | 55° 16´ N | 08° 15´ W | 313.5 |

Satellites give up the ghost eventually like all space vehicles, but there is a scheme for the replacement of the existing ones by a new generation in the next century. This time it will be paid for by a combination of public and private finance, with the United States Air Force and the Rockwell Corporation spending a total of $382 million on the project. What is not known is whether the replacement 24-hour positioning system will be free of charge, for while we have been the beneficiaries of a Cold War provision that outlived its military basis this cannot be relied on in the years to come.

# Appendix 1 • List of Geodetic Systems

*(See page 93 for the first ten common geodetic numbers)*

11  Adindan (Mean for Ethiopia and Sudan)
12  ARC 1950 (Mean for Botswana, Lesotho, Malawi, Swaziland, Zaire, Zambia, Zimbabwe)
13  Australian Geodetic 1984 (Australia)
14  Bermuda 1957 (Bermuda Islands)
15  Bogota Observatory (Columbia)
16  Campo Inchauspe (Argentina)
17  Chatham 1971 (Chatham Island)
18  Chua Astro (Paraguay)
19  Corrego Alegre (Brazil)
20  Djakarta (Batavia) (Sumatra)
21  European 1979 (Europe)
22  Geodetic Datum 1949 (New Zealand)
23  Guam 1963 (Guam)
24  Hayford 1910 (Finland)
25  Hjorsey 1955 (Iceland)
26  Indian (India and Nepal)
27  Ireland 1965 (Ireland)
28  Kertau 1948 (West Malaysia and Singapore)
29  L.C.5. Astro (Cayman Brac Island)
30  Liberia 1964 (Liberia)
31  Luzon (Philippines, excluding Mindanao)
32  Merchich (Morocco)
33  Minna (Cameroon)
34  Nahrwan (Oman)
35  Naparima, BWI (Trinidad and Tobago)
36  Old Egyptian (Egypt)
37  Old Hawaiian (Hawaiian Islands)
38  Pico De Las Nieves (Canary Islands)
39  Provisional South American 1956 (Mean for Bolivia, Chile, Columbia, Ecuador, Guyana, Peru, Venezuela)
40  Provisional South Chilean 1963 (Southern Chile)

41   Puerto Rico (Puerto Rico and Virgin Islands)
42   Qornoq (Southern Greenland)
43   RT90 (Sweden)
44   Santa Braz (Sao Miguel and Santa Maria Islands)
45   South American 1969 (Mean for Argentina, Bolivia, Brazil, Chile, Columbia, Ecuador, Guyana, Paraguay, Peru, Trinidad & Tobago, Venezuela)
46   Southwest Base (Graciosa Base) (Faial, Graciosa, Pico, Sao Jorge and Terceira Island)
47   Timbalai 1948 (Brunei and East Malaysia)
50   Adindan (Burkina Faso)
51   Adindan (Cameroon)
52   Adindan (Ethiopia)
53   Adindan (Mali)
54   Adindan (Senegal)
55   Adindan (Sudan)
56   Afgooye (Somalia)
57   Ain el Abd 1970 (Bahrain)
58   Ain el Abd 1970 (Saudi Arabia)
59   Ain el Abd 1970 (Cocos Islands)
60   Antigua Island Astro 1943 (Antigua and Leeward Islands)
61   Arc 1950 (Botswana)
62   Arc 1950 (Burundi)
63   Arc 1950 (Lesotho)
64   Arc 1950 (Malawi)
65   Arc 1950 (Swaziland)
66   Arc 1950 (Zaire)
67   Arc 1950 (Zambia)
68   Arc 1950 (Zimbabwe)
69   Arc 1950 (Mean for Kenya and Tanzania)
70   Ascension Island 1958 (Ascension Island)
71   Astro Beacon E 1945 (Iwo Jima)
72   Astro DOS 71/4 (St Helena Island)
73   Astro Tern Island 1961 (Tern Island)
74   Astronomical Station 1952 (Marcus Island)
75   Ayabelle Lighthouse (Djibouti)
76   Bellevue (IGN) (Efate and Erromango Islands)
77   Bissau (Guinea, Bissau)
78   Bukit Rimpah (Indonesia (Bangka and Belitung Islands))

79  Camp Area Astro (Antarctica (McMurdo Camp))
80  Canton Astro 1966 (Phoenix Islands)
81  Cape (South Africa)
82  Cape Canaveral (Bahamas and Florida)
83  Carthage (Tunisia)
84  Dabola (Guinea)
85  DOS 1968 (New Georgia Islands)
86  Easter Island 1967 (Easter Island)
87  European 1950 (Mean for Austria, Denmark, Germany, Netherlands, Switzerland)
88  European 1950 (Mean for Iraq, Israel, Jordan, Lebanon, Kuwait, Saudi Arabia, Syria)
89  European 1950 (Cyprus)
90  European 1950 (Egypt)
91  European 1950 (England, Channel Islands, Scotland, Shetland Islands)
92  European 1950 (Finland, Norway)
93  European 1950 (Greece)
94  European 1950 (Iran)
95  European 1950 (Italy (Sardinia))
96  European 1950 (Italy (Sicily))
97  European 1950 (Malta)
98  European 1950 (Portugal, Spain)
99  European 1979 (Mean for Austria, Finland, Netherlands, Norway, Spain, Sweden, Switzerland)
100  Fort Thomas 1955 (Nevis, St Kitts (Leeward Islands))
101  Gan 1970 (Maldives)
102  Guam 1963 (Guam)
103  Gunung Segara (Indonesia (Kalimantan))
104  GUX 1 Astro (Guadalcanal Island)
105  Herat North (Afghanistan)
106  Hong Kong 1963 (Hong Kong)
107  Hu-Tzu-Shan (Taiwan)
108  Indian (Bangladesh)
109  Indian 1954 (Thailand, Vietnam)
110  Indian 1975 (Thailand)
111  ISTS 061 Astro 1968 (South Georgia Islands)
112  ISTS 073 Astro 1969 (Diego Garcia)
113  Johnston Island 1961 (Johnston Island)
114  Kandawala (Sri Lanka)

115 Kerguelen Island 1949 (Kerguelen Island)
116 Kusaie Astro 1951 (Caroline Islands)
117 Legion Ghana
118 Luzon Philippines (Philippines Mindanoa)
119 Mahe 1971 (Mahe Island)
120 Massawa (Ethiopia (Eritrea))
121 Midway Astro 1961 (Midway Island)
122 Minna (Nigeria)
123 Montserrat Island Astro 1958 (Montserrat (Leeward Islands))
124 M'Poraloko (Gabon)
125 Nahrwan (Saudi Arabia)
126 Nahrwan (United Arab Emirates)
127 North American 1927 (NAD27) (Mean for Antigua, Barbados, Barbuda, Caicos Islands, Cuba, Dominican Republic, Grand Cayman, Jamaica, Turks Islands)
128 North American 1927 (NAD27) (Mean for Belize, Costa Rica, El Salvador, Guatemala, Honduras, Nicaragua)
129 North American 1927 (NAD27) (Mean for CONUS (East of Mississippi River))
130 North American 1927 (NAD27) (Mean for CONUS (West of Mississippi River))
131 North American 1927 (NAD27) (Alaska)
132 North American 1927 (NAD27) (Bahamas (Except San Salvador Island))
133 North American 1927 (NAD27) (Canada (Alberta, British Columbia))
134 North American 1927 (NAD27) (Canada (Manitoba, Ontario))
135 North American 1927 (NAD27) (Canada (New Brunswick, Newfoundland, Nova Scotia, Quebec))
136 North American 1927 (NAD27) (Canada (Northwest Territories, Saskatchewan))
137 North American 1927 (NAD27) (Canada (Yukon))
138 North American 1927 (NAD27) (Canal Zone)
139 North American 1927 (NAD27) (Cuba)
140 North American 1927 (NAD27) (Greenland (Hayes Peninsula))
141 North American 1927 (NAD27) (Mexico)
142 North American 1983 (Alaska, Canada, CONUS)

143  North American 1983 (Central America, Mexico)
144  Obersvatorio Metereo 1939 (Azores)
145  Old Hawaiian (Mean for Hawaii, Kauai, Maui, Oahu)
146  Old Hawaiian (Kauai)
147  Old Hawaiian (Maui)
148  Old Hawaiian (Oahu)
149  Oman (Oman)
150  Ordnance Survey of Great Britain 1936 (Mean for England, Isle of Man, Scotland, Shetland Islands, Wales)
151  Ordnance Survey of Great Britain 1936 (England, Isle of Man, Wales)
152  Ordnance Survey of Great Britain 1936 (Scotland, Shetland Islands)
153  Ordnance Survey of Great Britain 1936 (Wales)
154  Pitcairn Astro 1967 (Pitcairn Island)
155  Point 58 (Mean for Burkina Faso and Niger)
156  Pointe Noire 1948 (Congo)
157  Porto Santo 1936 (Porto Santo, Madeira Islands)
158  Provisional South American 1956 (Bolivia)
159  Provisional South American 1956 (Chile (Northern Near 19°S))
160  Provisional South American 1956 (Chile (Southern Near 43°S))
161  Provisional South American 1956 (Columbia)
162  Provisional South American 1956 (Ecuador)
163  Provisional South American 1956 (Guyana)
164  Provisional South American 1956 (Peru)
165  Provisional South American 1956 (Venezuela)
166  Qatar National (Qatar)
167  Reunion (Mascarene Islands)
168  Rome 1940 (Italy, Sardinia)
169  Santa(DOS) 1965 (Espirito Santo Island)
170  Sapper Hill 1943 (East Falkland Island)
171  Schwarzeck (Namibia)
172  Selvagem Grande (Salvage Islands)
173  SGS 85 Soviet Geodetic System 1985 (Russia)
174  South American 1969 (Argentina)
175  South American 1969 (Bolivia)
176  South American 1969 (Brazil)
177  South American 1969 (Chile)

178  South American 1969 (Columbia)
179  South American 1969 (Ecuador)
180  South American 1969 (Ecuador (Baltra, Galapagos))
181  South American 1969 (Guyana)
182  South American 1969 (Paraguay)
183  South American 1969 (Peru)
184  South American 1969 (Trinidad & Tobago)
185  South American 1969 (Venezuela)
186  South Asia (Singapore)
187  Tananarive Observatory 1925 (Madagascar)
188  Tokyo (Japan)
189  Tokyo (Korea)
190  Tokyo (Okinawa)
191  Tristan Astro 1968 (Tristan de Cunha)
192  Viti Levu 1916 (Fiji (Viti Levu Island))
193  Wake-Eniwetok 1960 (Marshall Islands)
194  Wake Island Astro 1952 (Wake Atoll)
195  Yacare (Uruguay)
196  Zanderij (Suriname)
197  Reserved
198  Reserved
199  Reserved
200  User Defined

**LORAN-C DATA (1)**

Sets with dual purpose GPS/Loran-C input may offer the following GRI numbers. They are listed in ascending numerical order.

| GRI Number | Chain/Station |
| --- | --- |
| 5930 | Canadian East Coast |
| 5980 | Attu Chayka |
| 5990 | Canadian West Coast |
| 6731 | Lessay (France) |
| 6780 | China |
| 7001 | Bo (Norway) |
| 7030 | Saudi Arabia South |
| 7270 | Newfoundland West Coast |
| 7430 | China North Sea |
| 7499 | Sylt (Germany) |
| 7950 | Chayka East Asia |
| 7960 | Gulf of Alaska |
| 7980 | South East USA |
| 7990 | Mediterranean Sea |
| 8000 | Western CIS |
| 8290 | North Central USA |
| 8830 | Saudi Arabia North |
| 8930 | North West Pacific |
| 8970 | Great Lakes |
| 9007 | Ejde (Faroes) |
| 9610 | South Central USA |
| 9930 | Korea |
| 9940 | West Coast USA |
| 9960 | Northwest USA |
| 9990 | North Pacific |

*LORAN-C*
*DATA (2)*

The nations subscribing to NELS, the North-west European Loran Service, are France, Germany, Denmark, Norway, Ireland and the Netherlands. The projected full list of NELS stations is:

| | |
|---|---|
| Jan Mayen | |
| Ejde | (Faroes) |
| Bo | (Norway) |
| Vaerlandet | (Norway) |
| Sylt | (Germany) |
| Lessay | (France) |
| Soustons | (France) |
| Loop Head | (Ireland) |

# Glossary

**Acquisition**  The process whereby the receiving set locates the satellite and begins to get useful data from it.

**Almanac**  Information about the satellite's time over the horizon, time of setting, elevation and direction.

**Alphanumeric**  Mixed letters and figures in a keyed entry.

**Altitude**  Height of the antenna above sea level. See also *Elevation.*

**Antenna**  The aerial that receives transmissions.

**Atomic clocks**  Fitted in satellites to give the precise time of a transmitted signal.

**Auto Mag**  An automatic adjustment for variation made by GPS sets so that they deliver magnetic courses and bearings unless told otherwise.

**Azimuth**  Bearing of an object in 360° notation; the direction of a satellite.

**Baseline extension**  A cause of error with Loran-C arising from greater width between Time Differences when in line with a master and a slave station.

**Bearing**  Direction of an object from observer or the direction between waypoints. Can be expressed as true or magnetic.

**CHAYKA**  The Russian equivalent of Loran-C.

**Clock bias**  The difference between a clock's indicated time and Universal Time Coordinated.

**Coarse**  (or **Course**) The standard GPS code for civilian users. **Acquisition** (C/A)  Signals from satellites are deliberately degraded to give position fixes with small amounts of error.

**Control segment**  The master control centre at Colorado Springs and other monitor and ground stations throughout the world.

**Course Deviation Indicator (CDI)**  Gives information about cross track error in graphic form.

**Courseline**  A planned line of travel from point of departure to destination. Called the track in orthodox navigation.

**Course Made Good** (CMG)  The course achieved by a vessel.

**Course Over Ground** (COG)   The direction of travel achieved. May not be the courseline.

**Course to steer**   The recommended course to rejoin a courseline.

**Cross track error** (XTE or XTK)   The perpendicular distance between present position and the courseline.

**Cursor**   Flashing symbol showing where data is to be entered or options may be changed, or a graphic location of the craft on a screen.

**Department of Defense**   The American controllers of GPS. Often shortened to DoD.

**Differential GPS** (DGPS)   A system based on land stations correcting the effects of Selective Availability to give sets fitted with special equipment a more accurate fix.

**Dilution of Precision** (DOP)   The measure of quality of satellite geometry and, hence, the accuracy of a fix.

**Distance Made Good** (DMG)   The distance from departure point, last position or waypoint to present position.

**Elevation**   Height of satellite above horizon or antenna above sea level.

**Ephemeris**   Data relating to the orbital parameters of satellites.

**Eurofix**   An experimental combination of GPS, Loran-C and radiobeacons to defeat Selective Availability.

**European Radionavigation Plan**   Proposed combination of GPS, GLONASS, Loran-C and CHAYKA to provide  more accurate fixes.

**FERNS**   The Far Eastern Radionavigation Service which brings together Loran-C provision in the Pacific area.

**First start**   See *Initialization*.

**Fix**   A single position in terms of latitude and longitude.

**Geodetic systems**   A scaling device to put coordinates on a chart or map and based on a particular datum.

**Geometric Dilution of Precision** (GDOP)   Another term for *Dilution of Precision*. Geometric Quality has a similar meaning.

**GLONASS**   The Russian equivalent of GPS.

**GNSS**   The projected Global Navigation Satellite System combining GPS and GLONASS.

**Ground Speed**   *Speed over the ground*, or actual speed over the sea, as opposed to speed through the water. *Velocity*

*over the ground* has the same meaning.

**Group Repetition Intervals**   A four-figure number identifying Loran-C chains.

**Hard keys**   Those having a single meaning, such as ENT or CLR.

**Horizontal Dilution of Precision** (HDOP)   Describes *Dilution of Precision* and often appears on status displays. It is a measure of accuracy.

**Initialization**   Telling a GPS set roughly where it is to reduce cold start time.

**Ionosphere**   A band of charged particles encircling the earth about 100 miles up that imparts small amounts of error to satellite signals.

**Leading zeroes**   Noughts put, for example, in front of low longitude numbers to avoid confusing a set that is not able to cope with blank spaces.

**Lock-on**   When a receiver has contact with satellites and can update its position continuously it has 'locked-on'. Lock-on-time is the interval between switch on and the receipt of a good set of signals.

**Mask angle**   A satellite is at mask angle when it is so close to the horizon that the GPS set gives up trying to get a position from it. Masking describes the blotting out of a signal by trees, tall structures, sails or high land.

**Nanosecond**   A thousandth of a millionth of a second.

**National Maritime Electronics Association** (NMEA)   The American organization that sets standards for compatibility of electronic equipment by means of numbered labels.

**Navstar Global Positioning System**   The full title of GPS.

**North-west European Loran Service** (NELS)   A union of France, Germany, Denmark, Norway, Ireland and the Netherlands providing a comprehensive Loran-C service.

**Page**   The screen on a GPS set.

**Protected (or Precision) Code (P-Code)**   The signal that the American military use. It is not subject to Selective Availability.

**Proximity alarm**   Sounds when your craft has penetrated the alarm circle around a waypoint.

**Pseudo-random code**   A succession of noughts and ones sent out by a satellite and compared to a similar code at the

receiver to give a time difference, and thus a position line. Pseudo-range is the distance found from these signals.

**Route**   A series of waypoints in order of use.

**Satellite Information Number**   A number identifying each satellite and used when status is being determined.

**Scrolling**   Repeated presses of a key to bring up fresh data.

**Selective Availability**   A signal being deliberately distorted to give error is said to be subject to Selective Availability and becomes a Coarse Acquisition, or civilian, signal. See also *Standard Positioning Service*.

**Signal-to-Noise Ratio**   A measure of the useful and non-useful parts of a signal.

**Soft keys**   Differently shaped from Hard Keys, or made of another material, and having more than one function.

**Space segment**   The satellite part of the GPS network.

**Speed of Advance** (SOA)   The vector component of ground speed in the direction of the destination waypoint.

**Speed Over the Ground** (SOG)   Has the same meaning as *Ground Speed* or *Velocity Over the Ground*.

**Standard Positioning Service**   The service provided to civilian users.

**Start-up**   See *Initialization*.

**Status**   An assessment of the strength, reliability and usefulness of a signal from a satellite.

**Time Differences**   Time between transmission and receipt that may be turned into a range.

**Unhealthy**   A satellite that has developed a fault is declared unhealthy and is ignored by the GPS set.

**Universal Time Coordinated** (UTC or UT)   An ultra-accurate version of Greenwich Mean Time.

**User segment**   The receivers, processors and antennae that permit an operator to receive signals.

**Velocity Made Good**   The speed of closing a selected waypoint.

**Velocity over the Ground** (VOG)   See *Ground Speed* and *Speed Over the Ground*.

**Waypoint**   A position on the earth's surface that you want to get to, or return to, in terms of latitude and longitude.

**World Geodetic System 84**   The highest grade of chart datum. If a chart bears this label, the positions found by GPS are likely to be highly accurate.

# *Index*